St. Louis Community
College

Library

5801 Wilson Avenue
St. Louis, Missouri 63110

WELFARE REFORM

Consensus or Conflict?

Edited by
James S. Denton

Foreword by
Daniel P. Moynihan

UNIVERSITY
PRESS OF
AMERICA

National
Forum
Foundation

Lanham • New York • London

Copyright © 1988 by

University Press of America,® Inc.

4720 Boston Way
Lanham, MD 20706

3 Henrietta Street
London WC2E 8LU England

British Cataloging in Publication Information Available

Co-published by arrangement with the National Forum Foundation

"The Neglected Cultural Frontier of Public Policy"
© 1988 by Michael Novak

"Old Dilemmas, New Directions"
© 1988 by Leslie Lenkowsky

"Family, Work, and Welfare Reform"
© 1988 by Carl A. Anderson

Library of Congress Cataloging-in-Publication Data

Welfare reform : consensus or conflict? / edited by James S. Denton :
foreword by Daniel P. Moynihan.
p. cm.
1. Public welfare—United States. 2. United States—Social
policy. I. Denton, James S.
HV95.W455   1988
361'.973—dc 19   88–14388 CIP
ISBN 0–8191–6902–1 (alk. paper)
ISBN 0–8191–6903–X (pbk. : alk. paper)

TABLE OF CONTENTS

FOREWORD

Daniel Patrick Moynihan

Some years ago, the Mayor of New York City, arguably the principal city of the world, and surely a symbol throughout the world of wealth and the display thereof, convened a panel of assorted wise persons and commanded them to peer into the not all that distant future of the year 2000. What would the city be like? What could be done to ensure its yet greater glory, higher eminence?

The report of the Commission, which appeared in 1987, came as something of a surprise. The richest city on earth faced a problem of poverty that threatened the very fabric of the City's life.

> Without a response to the problem of poverty, the New York of the 21st century will be not just a city divided, not just a city excluding those at the bottom from the fullness of opportunity, but a city in which peace and social harmony may not be possible. There is no more important issue for city government, no more important test for New York. (*New York Ascendant: Report of the Commission on the Year 2000,* June 1987.)

The impress of the Commission report was compounded, for some at least, by the realization that—beginning with the 20th century—New York City had been the focus of an extraordinary concern about poverty and ways to overcome and be done with it.

Scarcely a major social program adopted in Washington, D.C. during this century did not somehow first begin in New York City or State, sometimes merely as an idea, but just as often as a city or state program. This, after all, was Teddy Roosevelt's New York, Al Smith's New York, Franklin D. Roosevelt's New York. Here we see the beginning of labor legislation, housing programs, health programs, affirmative action race relations, intensive efforts at community organization and self help.

The very model for the community action programs associated with the "War on Poverty" that was launched from Washington in the 1960s came from a juvenile delinquency program begun on the lower east side of Manhattan. (See my *Maximum Feasible Misunderstanding, Community Action in the War on Poverty,* pp. 38-60, 1969.) And yet, somehow matters worsened.

The year after the Mayor's Commission reported, the President of the United States turned to this issue in his 1988 State of the Union Address. Calling for the welfare reform, President Reagan commented:

> My friends, some years ago, the Federal Government declared war on poverty, and poverty won. . . .
>
> Too often it has only made poverty harder to escape. Federal welfare programs have created a massive social problem. With the best of intentions, government created a poverty trap that wreaks havoc on the very support system the poor need most to lift themselves out of poverty—the family. Dependency has become the one enduring heirloom, passed from one generation to the next, of too many fragmented families.
>
> It is time—this may be the most radical thing I've said in 7 years in this office—it is time for Washington to show a little humility. There are a thousand sparks of genius in 50 States and a thousand communities around the Nation. It is time to nurture them and see which ones can catch fire and become guiding lights.
>
> States have begun to show us the way. They have demonstrated that successful welfare programs can be built around more effective child support enforcement practices and innovative programs requiring welfare recipients to work or prepare for work.

The President is quite correct in calling attention to the energy and creativity with which State governments have addressed the issue of welfare dependency in recent years. As Senators will know, last year the National Governors Association made welfare reform its number one issue. Governors Clinton of Arkansas, then Chairman of the Association, and Governor Castle of Delaware brought their proposal to the Finance Committee, and we fashioned our bill (S. 1511) after their model. Time and again I have referred to it as the Governors' Bill.

I emphasize my agreement with the President in this large matter, as I would beg to differ on the lesser point with which he opened his discussion. Which is to say that in the War on Poverty, "poverty won."

It happens I was present in the Rose Garden at midmorning of August 20, 1964, on the occasion President Johnson signed the Economic Opportunity Act of 1964. These were his opening remarks:

> On this occasion the American people and our American system are making history.

> For so long as man has lived on this earth poverty has been his curse.

> On every continent in every age men have sought escape from poverty's oppression.

> Today for the first time in all the history of the human race, a great nation is able to make and is willing to make a commitment to eradicate poverty among its people.

At no point in his remarks that day did he use the term "war on poverty," but that usage became common and President Reagan surely reflects a widespread judgment that as a nation we failed in that great undertaking.

Not long ago, a cover story in *U.S. News & World Report,* by the able young scholar David Whitman, noted that Tom Fletcher, the impoverished coal miner President Johnson visited in a vastly publicized tour of Eastern Kentucky, is still poor, still living in the same cabin. Just this week an editorial in *The New Republic,* commenting on a decline in the quality of American civic culture, notes:

> One of the causes is the frustration of grinding poverty, particularly in the wake of both insincere promises and oafish efforts to end it.

Indeed, some of the more eccentric programs of the time aroused considerable opposition. Osborn Elliott recently noted that in his final State of the Union message, President Johnson did not even mention the Great Society and anti-poverty programs.

There were, you could say, auguries. I sat beside Sargent Shriver on March 17, 1964 as he presented the opening testimony on the Economic Opportunity Act before the House Committee on Education and Labor. When at length Chairman Powell invited the comment of a senior Republican member, the hapless legislator could only offer us a reading from John 12:18: "For the poor always ye have with you."

In the near quarter century since, this prophecy appears to have been borne out. About one American in six was poor in 1964. About one in six is poor today.

However, I would offer the thought that this seeming intractable proportion is the result of two quite opposite movements.

In 1964, poverty was essentially a problem of the aged. More than a quarter of the aged were poor.

But programs enacted under President Johnson and President Nixon primarily within the Social Security area, greatly reduced poverty among the elderly. I refer especially to Medicare, to SSI, and to the increase and subsequent indexing of Old Age Insurance benefits.

PERCENTAGE BELOW POVERTY LINE

	1966	1986
65 AND OVER	28.5%	12.4%

Source: U.S. Census Bureau

This is a wholly unacceptable level of poverty among the aged. Even so it is a much reduced level, and this was anticipated.

By contrast, of a sudden we look up to find there are more poor Americans today than a quarter century ago, and that the poorest group in our population are children!

Moreover, in actual numbers and as a proportion of the age group—one in five—poverty is greater among children today than it was a quarter century ago.

As we approach the end of the 20th century, a child in America is almost twice as likely to be poor as an adult!

This is a condition that has never before existed in our history. Most probably, it has never before existed in the history of the human species.

PERCENTAGE BELOW POVERTY LINE
1986

AGE GROUP	
UNDER 18 YEARS	19.8%
18-64	11.1
65 AND OVER	12.4

Source: U.S. Census Bureau

How has this come about? At one level the answer is simple. It is, as Samuel H. Preston put it in the 1984 Presidential Address to the Population Association of America: "the earthquake that shuddered through the American family in the past twenty years." The twenty years, that is, from the beginning of the poverty program.

Which is to say a *new poverty problem* has emerged.

As the Census has just reported, in 1986, nearly one in every four (23.5 percent) children lived with only one parent, two and one half times the proportion in 1960. The vast majority (89 percent) of these 14.8 million children lived with their mothers. These include 18.3 percent of all white children, 53.1 percent of all black children, and 30.4 percent of all Hispanic children.

CHILDREN UNDER 18 LIVING WITH ONE PARENT

	1986	1960
TOTAL	23.5%	9.1%
WHITE	18.3	7.1
BLACK	53.1	21.9
HISPANIC	30.4	(NA)

Source: U.S. Census Bureau

Estimates of the number of children who will live with a single parent at some point during childhood are yet more striking. Arthur Norton of the U.S. Bureau of the Census predicts that 61 percent of children born in 1987 will live for some time with only one biological parent before reaching 18. Inevitably, large numbers of these children require some form of public assistance.

Further, in providing such assistance, *we have created an extraordinary institutional bias against minority children.*

The Social Security Act has two provisions for the care of children in single parent families. The first is Aid to Families with Dependent Children, enacted into law as part of the original 1935 Social Security Act. The second is Survivors Insurance, added to the Act in 1939. The characteristics of these two populations are quite different. The majority of the children receiving SI benefits are white. The majority of the children receiving AFDC are black or Hispanic.

RACIAL COMPOSITION OF AFDC AND SURVIVORS
Insurance Caseloads

	SI	AFDC
WHITE	66%	40%
BLACK	22	41
HISPANIC	8	14
OTHER	4	5

Source: Social Security Administration and Family Support Administration; AFDC data are for 1986; SI data are estimated for 1985.

Since 1970 we have *increased* the real benefits received by children under SI by *53 percent!*

We have *cut* the benefits of AFDC children by *13 percent*!

The United States Government, the American people, now provide a child receiving SI benefits almost *three times* what we provide a child on AFDC!

To those who say we don't care about children in our country, may I note that the average provision for children under SI has been rising five times as fast as average family income since 1970.

We do care about some children. Majority children.

It is minority children—not only but mostly—who are left behind.

AVERAGE MONTHLY AFDC AND SURVIVORS INSURANCE
Benefits Payments
(Per Recipient Payment, in Constant 1986 Dollars)

	SI	AFDC
1970	$222	$140
1986	$339	$122
% Change	+ 53%	-13%

Source: Social Security Administration and Family Support Administration

In terms of the present emphasis on education in the President's
State of the Union, consider this table of the proportion of
children in major urban school districts who are *now* on welfare.
(Consider how much greater that proportion would be if measured
over time.)

PERCENTAGE OF CHILDREN ENROLLED IN
PUBLIC SCHOOLS ON AFDC
(By Selected Cities**)

Hartford	58%
Newark	58%
New York	45%
Detroit	45%
Chicago	44%
Oakland	43%
Gary, Indiana	42%
Philadelphia	42%
Jackson, Miss.	40%
Minneapolis	33%
New Orleans	31%
Seattle	31%

(By Selected Cities in New York State**)

Utica	50%
Buffalo	47%
New York	45%
Rochester	38%
Niagara Falls	33%
Yonkers	32%

**The data in these tables were provided by city officials.

Remember these children on average receive less support today than they did 20 years ago. Is it any great wonder, on the edge of privation or worse, that they do not become model scholars?

Surely, if someone in that Rose Garden a quarter century ago had predicted we would treat our children so, the rest of us would have predicted the troubles the children now have.

Why has this come about? Why this institutional bias?

I believe we know why. Welfare has become a stigmatized program. Children dependent on it—as many as one child in three before reaching 18—are stigmatized as well. That surely is what institutional bias means.

The problem—and clearly we have difficulty grasping this—is that welfare recipients are stigmatized and welfare programs are undersupported because their beneficiaries are somehow seen as undeserving. How a two year old child can be so depicted, I do not understand. Yet, there you have it.

In 1973, I began an account of President Nixon's effort to establish a guaranteed income (the Family Assistance Plan) with these words:

> The issue of welfare is the issue of dependency. It is different from poverty. To be poor is an objective condition; to be dependent, a subjective one as well. That the two circumstances interact is evident enough, and it is no secret that they are frequently combined. Yet a distinction must be made. Being poor is often associated with considerable personal qualities; being dependent rarely so. This is not to say that dependent people are not brave, resourceful, admirable, but simply that their situation is never enviable, and rarely admired. It is an incomplete state in life: normal in the child, abnormal in the adult. In a world where completed men and women stand on their own feet, persons who are dependent—as the buried imagery of the word denotes—hang.

Fifteen years later I see no grounds for changing a single word.

Do we understand how deep this prejudice is? Or if you like, presumption. From the time the British began experimenting with "manhood suffrage" it was clearly understood that no one receiving welfare could possibly expect the right to vote. A statute of 1832 specifically denied the franchise to any male receiving parish relief, as it was then known. John Stuart Mill thought the matter self evident:

> . . . the receipt of parish relief should be a peremptory disqualification for the franchise. He who cannot by his labour suffice for his own support, has no claim to the privilege of helping himself to the money of others. By becoming dependent on the remaining members of the community for actual subsistence, he abdicates his claim to equal rights with them in other respects. (John Stuart Mill, *Essays on Politics and Society,* University of Toronto Press, 1977, p. 472.)

In fact, the statute that prohibited those receiving relief or other alms from voting was not repealed until 1910! Women, at least those who were not on poor relief, were granted suffrage in 1918. Today, in the United States, we might as well live in Mill's England, for the welfare poor of this country don't vote either.

And yet, there is some progress to report. We have, in the United States, begun to find some common ground. A consensus, slow to form, yet indisputably there, has emerged: We must help those people who are able to become independent.

Toward this end, we further agree that parents must assume responsibility for their children. Fathers must contribute to their children's financial upkeep and mothers may have to help out by working.

Whether parents divorce, separate, or fail to wed does not change the essential fact: Both parents must care for their children. The absent parent, usually the father, must systematically contribute child support payments. The custodial parent, usually the mother, must prepare herself to find and keep a job, at least part-time. To the extent that parental income, from both parents, is still insufficient, then government must lend a hand.

Congress is trying to translate these principles into legislation to reform our half-century old AFDC program. If we succeed, we will have taken an important first step toward helping the nation's children. Oddly, we seem to encounter the most serious opposition from those who claim to advocate for the poor. They argue that anything less than guaranteed incomes and guaranteed jobs and guaranteed child care and health care (with no strings attached) is unacceptable.

Some of us find this baffling. In an era of grotesque deficits and staggering national debt, we would be thankful to redefine "welfare," to take those first but crucial steps of securing parental support for children, providing education and training for their parents who need and want to work, providing benefits for poor children who live with both their parents, and providing transitional assistance with child and health care for parents who succeed in leaving the welfare rolls for payrolls.

The authors whose work appears in these pages are serious and informed. With the help of their insights, those of us toiling in the legislative arena may yet succeed in reforming welfare.

INTRODUCTION

James S. Denton

It is nearly impossible today to remember the enthusiasm that greeted President Lyndon Johnson's call for a War on Poverty. The cynicism and bitterness that are now wrapped around the term itself were barely specks on the horizon in the weeks following Johnson's 1964 speech. Most Republicans in Congress did not even seriously try to impede the passage of the Economic Opportunity Act, so broad was the popularity of a campaign to end poverty in the midst of plenty.

By one measure, the War on Poverty has succeeded beyond anything its architects might have hoped for. Government spending on the poor is now higher than anyone envisioned in the early 1960s. The $132 billion spent on the 59 major federal welfare programs in 1985 is six times greater, in constant dollars, than all state and federal welfare expenditures in 1960. This rapid growth did not take place in response to a broad economic crisis, as did the establishment and expansion of relief programs in the 1930s. America was a wealthy country in 1960, and an even wealthier one in 1985.

The point of all the new programs of the 1960s, Americans were told, was to end poverty, not to underwrite it forever at indefinitely higher levels. Not only has the government failed to eliminate poverty, it has not even made progress towards that goal that can be detected by the most basic measures. The portion of the American population living in poverty remained essentially constant, from twelve to thirteen percent, between 1968 and 1985.

To spend so much and accomplish so little is manifestly bad politics. It tests the patience of the taxpayers. It gives them little reason to suffer explanations about the complexities of the poverty problem or the relative success of individual programs. And it undermines faith in the basic competence of our government, not only to cure poverty, but to address any significant national priority.

Wasting money, a serious enough problem, is not the worst charge that can be made against our welfare system. The worst charge is that the billions we have spent on poverty have had a negative, not merely negligible, impact. A growing body of research suggests that the unintended consequences of our welfare programs include increased dependency on government, diminished ability and desire to be self-supporting through labor force participation, and insupportable strains on the cohesion of families.

The magnitude of these problems has engendered more creative thinking about what a beneficial welfare system must do. For years the debate on welfare has been simple—liberals wanted to spend more, conservatives wanted to spend less. Recently, both conservatives and liberals have been saying that the real need is to spend better. A consensus is emerging that a welfare system that spends money better can be built. The leading features of this welfare system include making the clearest possible distiction between people who cannot fend for themselves and those who can; developing government policies that assure a decent standard of living for the former; and developing policies that provide assistance and stern incentives for the latter to get them into the work force and stable families, and keep them there.

The appearance of similar articles in ideologically diverse journals hardly guarantees the imminent passage of welfare reform legislation. Enormous political inertia attaches to the status quo, notwithstanding its fundamental problems and embarrassing track record. The political beneficiaries of the present system include welfare recipients who are more afraid of changing than enduring the present system, politicians who gain votes by exploiting those fears, and government employees who have built careers around the administration of the welfare system in its present form.

Ordinarily, the opposition of such imposing political forces would be reason enough to give up on the prospects of welfare reform. We may take encouragement, however, from the knowledge that equally powerful forces were arrayed against tax reform in 1986. Their defeat showed that American democracy retains the ability to pursue the public interest, that special interests do not always have to get the final word on government policy.

One key to the success of tax reform was its vigorous support by a varied group of experts and activists. The welfare system, too, can be reformed, but not without a similar consensus among people who are equally persuasive and thoughtful. It bodes well for the future of welfare reform that just such people have contributed to this volume examining the problems and needs of our welfare system from a variety of perspectives. Their understanding of the need for a sober, realistic approach can help advance a clearly defined alternative to the present welfare system, one that appeals to the common sense and the common decency of the American people.

This book is offered as a vehicle for hastening the emergence of that consensus on the need for comprehensive reform of the welfare system. This consensus, skillfully articulated, can help overcome the political barriers to better welfare programs. A firm commitment to the values of work, family, and concern for the needy must characterize a sound approach to welfare reform. Such a commitment animates the individual articles that comprise this volume. It is a theme intended to be not only morally and intellectually satisfying, but politically consequential as well.

***

The National Forum Foundation gratefully acknowledges the support of its many members who made this book and the conference which preceeded it possible. Particular thanks is given to The Carthage Foundation, The Coors Foundation, The J.M. Foundation and The John M. Olin Foundation.

***

The editor wishes to acknowledge the insights and graciousness of the contributors to this volume, and the assistance of Dennis Smith, William Voegeli and Joseph Piccione in the stages of preparing this book for publication.

THE NEGLECTED CULTURAL FRONTIER OF PUBLIC POLICY

Michael Novak

It is important to try to weave together certain important themes which, lying in the background, are part of the serious reflection that many in this country are trying to conduct as we begin a new era in welfare policy, and begin a new experiment. Having evaluated or begun to evaluate the experiments we have tried these last twenty years, many on all sides are trying to launch a new beginning.

My approach has a theological character and will weave together seven points, unwrap seven seals, and touch on each one of them very briefly.

(1) *The first seal: Character.* The first seal is the return of the idea of character in the 1980s, what James Q. Wilson at Harvard calls the most arresting, deep and important event that he has experienced in the last twenty years. He did this in the 20th anniversary issue of *The Public Interest,* the return of the theme of character. Do we remember the American hymn, "Confirm Thy Soul in Self Control"? Go back to the McGuffey readers and read the social history of the 19th and early 20th century. You will be astonished to see how often the word "character" or its equivalents—"self-mastery," "self-discipline," "self-improve-

ment'' recur as basic motifs. Our rights, James Madison said, are not defined by words on parchment; their real defense lies in the habits and the institutions of the American people.

First, why was character so important? Teddy Roosevelt issued a maxim at least as often as he rode a horse, which was quite a lot. Even in the Depression, in my childhood, maxims were a heavy industry. Why? Because our founders deemed that an experiment in self government, government of the people, and by the people, depended on the capacity of each citizen to govern himself. If one cannot govern oneself, how can all of us collectively govern either ourselves or the republic? Character is necessary to release the *spiritual energy for self-government.* If we could not be responsible, we could not govern ourselves. As so many philosophers have thought it would, democracy would end in anarchy.

Secondly, character was necessary to provide the *spiritual energy for the novel American economy:* an economy based on the capacities of persons to launch their *own* enterprises. Oscar Handlin points out that in the year 1800, there being only 4 million people in the United States at the time—an infant nation—there were already more business corporations in the United States than in all of Britain, all of Europe, in fact the whole world combined.

This new ''order'' was an economy based on invention and discovery, whose fundamental idea is that the cause of the wealth of nations is invention. Wealth doesn't come from natural resources. Brazil has more resources than Japan and is poor. Japan has virtually no natural resources and yet produces 10% of the gross world product. Wealth comes from intellect, from invention and from discovery—entering into realms no one ever before imagined. To release that energy, a society needs persons of character, who are able to make decisions for themselves, to take responsibility for themselves, to bear the risk and the loss, and of course and above all, to know how to work with others.

What we most often forget is that capitalism is a *social* system. No one starts a business alone. Any enterprising person immediately depends upon others. That is why teamwork is our most important idea—or, as de Tocqueville expressed it, *association.* The habit of associations is very deep in the American character. As some of my colleagues in Europe have pointed out, Americans don't only work forty hours a week. They also go to almost forty hours of meetings a week—cub scouts, PTA, and the rest.

Thirdly, character is important in order to release the *energy of the moral-cultural system.* For the economic and political parts of our system depend on the capacities of its citizens. Apart from the virtues of its citizens (skills of moral and intellectual kinds), both the political system and the economic system fall apart. When we hit a decadent moment in our history, both fall apart very quickly.

Why, then, character being so important, was it forgotten? I won't now go back into history to offer a theory about that. But I think it is fair to say that within the last thirty or forty years or so, there's come to be—along with the literary modernism of the sort we began teaching in our colleges all over the country—a motif of *liberation*; above all, a liberation from burdens, especially from the burdens of the mind itself: Liberation to feel and to experience, but no longer to take responsibility for what we feel and experience, and for what we do with our feelings and experiences. The easy slippage from "I *judge* this is so" to "I *feel* this is so" represents a long step down.

Without going into all the reasons for it, let me point out as well that both among conservatives on the right and liberals on the left, there has been a systematic dislike of capitalism—a systematic putting down of the so-called "bourgeois" virtues, and character, and particularly of "bourgeois" tastes. Consider the language of class used in our universities. If somebody says to you, "You have bourgeois tastes," you should know enough to be insulted. How ironic that is, when most of the beautiful things in this world have been made by the bourgeoisie. Who makes the fine tablecloths? Not the nobility and not the peasants. Who made the silver, who did the tapestries, who were the first painters, who makes the best wine, who makes the best china? Most of the finest things are made in family shops in places like France and Italy. They are made by the first persons to own their own property, being neither lords nor aristocrats, neither from the well-born, nor from the peasants. To say that you have bourgeois tastes is both a put down, and is historically inaccurate. On the other hand, if someone should say to you, "You are a prince of a man," or "a princess," you are supposed to feel complimented. Although if you think a little bit about the history of princes and princesses—what murderers many were—what liars and cheats and how few human accomplishments they had, it's astonishing that such a bias should persist. One finds it, nonetheless, in literary criticisms of wealth, especially of non-aristocratic wealth, of the *nouveaux riches.*

Aristocrats of the right prefer the 18th century—before asphalt parking lots, McDonalds and massage parlors, and join company with the anti-bourgeois spirit of the left.

(2) *The second seal: Outside/In Theories.* As a result of the loss of this theme of character, and its absence from American life for twenty years or more, there came to be the dominance of what I should like to refer to as "outside/in" theories. This is the notion that the way to achieve social programs and to be progressive is to change the environment and ignore the interior. From 1960 to 1980, we gave a great deal of attention to changing the environment. Spending on social welfare to change that environment went from about $39 billion to $244 billion in that period. By 1976 after having built new programs directed precisely at youth, on the average of one a month since 1960, we had 260 such programs. And in this period, 1960-1980, the SAT scores fell on the average of four points a year, about 85 points. Births to teenagers, the very ones at whom the programs have been aimed, despite so much spending going on, jumped by almost 100%, notwithstanding the fact that pregnancies among teenagers are chiefly interrupted by abortion, which also jumped nearly 100%. During this period, deaths in autos by teenagers doubled, arrests of juveniles also doubled.

It is not unfair to say, even reading lightly over the literature, that many youths have sensed the absence of a path for their lives. The absence of a project, let's say of self-mastery. Earlier, self-mastery had been imagined as a lifetime project. A lifetime voyage. No longer. This is the only country in the world with practically a constitutional obligation to be happy. That's not enough. First of all, life is not mostly happiness. David Hume said that on the whole, he thought it was better not to marry, because there is more unhappiness in every life than happiness, so marrying would worsen your chances.

But you have a group of youngsters for whom there is no voyage to take, no character to develop, no paths to master, no goal to achieve, as they become 15, 17, 20, 30 and so forth: if nonetheless their lives are supposed to be happy, there is a meaninglessness that can soon come, which is hard to blot out even with very loud music.

(3) *The third seal: A misplaced debate.* There has come out of all of this, seeing that something is wrong with what we are doing, a powerful sense that we are not achieving the results that we all had intended to achieve. The debate over welfare policy is often described in terms of a misplaced debate. The debate was put in these terms: Shall we turn either to self-reliance or to the government for assistance? Isn't that really a jumbling of means and ends?

From the very beginning, *political* economy has always meant that one uses *government* to advance the general welfare. Use government, of course, but not to swamp persons in the process. Think of the Homestead Act. Our founders were determined not to imitate the pattern of Latin America, not to let the West develop in the pattern of large landed estates with a few aristocrats and many peons. They didn't want to let that happen. They wanted to open the country to as many landowners as possible, in part on Adam Smith's principle, that the wealth of nations is caused by intellect. Therefore, multiply the number of intellects making decisions, and you'll increase the magnitudes of intellect throughout the country. Without broad-based property rights you have that many fewer intellects making economic decisions. And of course, along with the Homestead Act went land grants for our colleges. Every new territory was obligated to open a university for exactly the same reason: wealth comes from intellect.

Note that these were *government* programs. Yet designed to liberate people. They were designed to empower a people of character, people who have intellects of their own; who can make their own decisions; do their own projects; make their own new discoveries, discover new resources of wealth, and the rest.

So, it's not *either* self-reliance *or* the government. It is using government as a means to help attain self-reliance, to help develop character and to liberate people of character. Then you can have government of the people, by the people, for the people *when* the people are of a certain sort.

Martin Luther King, Jr. said this in one of his most famous phrases. "I have a dream—of the day when black children will be judged, *not* by the color of their skin," and here is the precise point, "*but by the content of their character.*" He hit it right on the button. In a way, he is one of the last voices of that older tradition, which saw at some points in American history as many as 55-60% of all the youngsters all across the country in Sunday Schools, learning precisely how to form their own character and how to make the formation of their own character one of the main acts of their creation in life.

(4) *The fourth seal: Culture in Public Policy.* When we think about public policy, we've all been trained to think that there are *two* main parts to it, the *political* part and the *economy. Political economy* is what that science—or, better, art—is now called. The canoniter of that term, Adam Smith, who was himself a moral philosopher, understood political economy to be a branch of morals. So did John Stuart Mill. But what that "morals" part is has been too often forgotten. So when we think about public policy, we tend to think about what the *government* can do, and what other political agencies besides government can do, and what the *economic* system can do. We fail to think of the third part of our system, the moral part, the part that we deliberately kept independent of the state: the press, the universities, the intellectuals, the churches, the artists, the free associations of many kinds who were responsible for shaping the intellectual and the moral form of the country. This part of our system is independent to a remarkable degree, from the state, from the political system and even from the economic system. Americans of different personality types, even in the same family, tend toward one of these three systems and not the others. It's meant to be that way.

Our founders put on our coins "In God We Trust," meaning, "nobody else." The defense of our liberties depends upon dividing the three systems.

We think too little about what the *culture* may do. Welfare reform is not only a challenge for the political system or the economic system. We have to ask: What are our cultural leaders doing? What are the teachers doing? Our journalists? The movie-makers? The TV producers? The preachers and clergy? Public relations executives? Advertisers? Parents? What is the weight of our culture? What are we telling our young people, as a culture? In that formative period of their lives when they depend on signals from others, what sort of signals have we been giving them?

Well I think we can see, at the very least, the signals they haven't been given. We have abandoned in the last twenty years the theme of character. Even to use that word would have, until recently, marked one as old-fashioned and subject to ridicule.

(5) *The fifth seal: The Rapidity of Cultural Change.* Next it is important to notice how rapidly all of this can change. I recently read in the newspaper Jesse Jackson's statement to youngsters at a high school: "You're not a man because you can make a baby, but because you can protect, provide, raise and love a baby." Now notice that phrase, "you're not a man." What does it mean? *Of course,* you're a man—biologically. But when we use the word "you're a man," we mean being a man is something you have to *live up to.* You have to be a man, not just biologically; rather, a man of a certain character. Showing courage, responsibility, foresight, wisdom. You can't act like a kid anymore. Becoming a man, becoming a woman, is a goal to be attained. That's what Jackson was saying. Not enough people are saying it. Carolyn Wallace, the social worker from Newark, told Bill Moyers, a TV interviewer electrifying the country, "If you say it on your corner, and I say it on my corner and everybody's saying it, it's going to be like a drum beat." And she meant, we need the powerful media to be saying: "No, don't have babies if you can't provide for them." Yet in a larger context, the drum beat says: "You've got to be a man! You've got to be a woman! You've got to have *character.*"

Otherwise, you're not capable of self-government for yourself; and the country's not capable of governing itself.

It is the responsibility of a culture to cultivate its own young and to give their lives at least a beginning shape. This is a very important task. We have not been allowing them to hear the needed drum beat. And when enough of us do, life will be much easier for the political system and for the economic system.

A smaller example. When I was at Harvard in the early 60s, there weren't such things as food stamps, and if there had been, and if we had taken food stamps in those days, our friends would have ridiculed us. And we would have felt ashamed. Because relief for the poor, we would have thought in those days, is not intended for Harvard students. Nowadays, that's changed. One meets youngsters from Harvard at Aspen, in Paris and Ft. Lauderdale and other hardship spots, receiving unemployment checks, to which they now feel they're fully entitled. When youngsters from Harvard do that, there's been a change in the *ethos,* in some twenty short years, which puts a tremendous burden on the political system, and which the political system wasn't intended to bear. And on the economic system as well. A change in the *ethos* can be very powerful.

(6) *The sixth seal: The Change in Family Structure.* A change in family structure, according to the Census Bureau, is the largest single new cause of poverty. In 1959 28% of American families were headed by single-parents, about 14.8 million persons. Today, single-parent families represent about 30.8 million persons. And there has been a net jump in the numbers of the poor of about 4.6 million persons simply by that change of family structure. Put otherwise, if we had the same proportion of single-parent households in 1984 as we had in 1959, we'd have about 4.6 million fewer poor persons. This is an important fact. It shows that there are kinds of poverty—in this case, the fastest growing kind of poverty—that arise from personal choices. Nobody forces people to abandon spouse, to separate, to divorce, or to have children outside of wedlock. The government doesn't. There's no law saying you have to do that. But on the other hand, the government can hardly stop you if you want to do it. If *you* make those choices,

and if millions of people make those choices, there are going to be consequences throughout the social system. These consequences will be borne in part by the individuals who make the choices, but also in part by the rest of society. There is a dimension to our concern about poverty that is due to the *ethos,* to the way we choose to live, the ethical patterns we choose to adopt.

Therefore, I argue if we think that this creates a problem, a weighty public expense, and a social task we need to address, we are obligated to examine its cultural dimensions. This change in U.S. family structure, further, comes at a time when there is more help for the poor, and when what counts as poverty is on a higher level, than ever before. Nonetheless, people are choosing ways of life that are bound to include more and more single parents and children among the poor. We haven't yet arrested this.

(7) *The seventh seal: The Cultural Dimension.* So, finally, let me conclude. Welfare reform is not solely a political problem, and it is not solely an economic problem, though of course it is that because we tend to define poverty in financial terms rather than in terms of the human spirit. But it is also a cultural problem.

There is something in our ethos, in our culture, that we ourselves have cumulatively chosen over the past twenty years, and in contra-distinction to what Americans in the past had chosen. This is something, then, that, God willing, we can also unchoose. To the extent that our own ethos is a matter of choice, we can learn, we can re-think, and we can change direction. That's the marvelous thing about cultural analysis. In the end, there's no one to blame but oneself. Because individuals can and do often change culture.

Public policy, in my view, includes encouraging reflection and action within and upon our cultural system—that drum beat that Carolyn Wallace talked about, that ethos of cumulative and consistent determination. The greatest power in the world is the power of the raised eyebrow. It is a power which tells our friends and our associates: "If you're going to associate with us, we don't approve of that kind of behavior." That was the power that, in the end, held together the neighborhood political machines of the past. You could say whatever you wanted, but when the ward leader raised his eyebrow, you fell silent. That's an often neglected form of power—cultural power. He would say with his eyebrow, in effect: that isn't the message coming out of this ward at this time.

"Who sent you?" the Democratic ward leader asked the young fellow from the University of Chicago looking to volunteer to work for Adlai Stevenson many years ago. The kid said, "Nobody sent me, I just wanted to help out. I want to volunteer." The ward leader took his cigar from his mouth and said: "Kid, we don't want nobody nobody sent."

Each of us needs social encouragement. And especially when you're young, you need encouragement. You need elders to tell you what to do because the great tragedy often comes when people make choices whose consequences they don't quite foresee. Tragedy arises when these consequences turn out to be opposite to what you wanted. Yet you made the choice, nobody else made it for you.

Youngsters are always in that position. They're always making choices about matters whose consequences they can't possibly know. After they live through them they will know, but then it is a little late. That is why a culture must supply encouragement for its young: must acculturate them. Such encouragement has always been best summarized in this country as character. That is the best moral goal a free people can aim at. For, once achieved, it allows persons to take reponsibility for their own actions. The skills that go into having character—the relevant emotions, the discernment, and the courage to act—represent the whole range of skills that make us admire a human being. When we see any one of those skills absent, we count it as among a person's character flaws, one of those inevitable faults each of us has.

Daily life obliges us to use the vocabulary of character all the time. And yet we have not very much encouraged one another for some time now, to attend to the national ethos, to pay attention to the moral character of our people as a whole. Yet the character of our people, their habits and institutions, are the chief vitalities upon which this country depends, in its political system, in its economic system and in its moral-cultural system; without which liberty is lost.

OLD DILEMMAS, NEW DIRECTIONS

Leslie Lenkowsky

A dramatic moment occurred twenty-two years ago on Capitol Hill. President Johnson had just announced his declaration of "war on poverty" and with great symbolism, had sent his predecessor's brother, Attorney General Robert F. Kennedy, to present the proposed Economic Opportunity Act to the House Committee on Education and Labor. The event seemed to mark the rebirth of the national spirit after mournful months that had followed President Kennedy's assassination. After making his opening remarks, the Chairman, Cong. Adam Clayton Powell, turned to the senior Republican present, who began by reciting from the Book of John: "For the poor always ye have with you."

Among many of those present, this performance struck a note of disbelief, no less than it would now. We have grown so accustomed to the idea that eliminating poverty is an urgent priority for American society, and for government in particular, that the proposition it might be a futile endeavor—even when backed by Biblical authority—seems unconvincing. Indeed, in his State of the Union message earlier this year, no less of a skeptic toward government social programs than Ronald Reagan joined every president since Kennedy in directing his staff and Cabinet officers to find new ways of assuring that far fewer of the poor are with us, as well he might following a period during which their number reached a twenty-year high.

To be sure, his aides will not have to come back with just the Scriptures. For we do know that there are some steps government can take to reduce poverty. Sound fiscal and monetary policies that produce a sustained period of economic growth, for example, will enable millions to escape poverty and many others to have a higher standard of living. This was, in fact, the main weapon in President Johnson's arsenal and we have seen more recent evidence of its potency in a sharp reduction in the official measure of poverty last year.

Government can also help the poor by not taxing them into deeper poverty. Yet, this is exactly what we have been doing and while tax reform legislation will greatly rectify that situation, the poor will still pay sizable amounts of their meager incomes for Social Security, as well as state and local levies.

Finally, there is that vast complex of government-provided services, ranging from education to economic development, from day care to health care, from public jobs to public housing, through which we try to help the poor acquire the skills and opportunities they need to get out of poverty. To put it mildly, how well these really work has been a matter of considerable dispute. Many who have looked carefully doubt they are cost-effective and in some cases, conclude they may have done more harm than good; others disagree, citing evidence such as the results of the Ypsilanti pre-school program, or the "workfare" demonstrations. Whatever the case, however, hardly anyone seriously believes that these programs could be mounted with sufficient skill and scope to do more than modestly diminish the ranks of the poor.

Even twenty years ago this was understood. Even while the programs of the "war on poverty" were being enacted and implemented, more than a few of its strategists suspected the expectations for them would vastly exceed their accomplishments. Many also realized that large numbers of the poor were too old, too young, too infirm, or too burdened by other responsibilities, such as child-care, to be able to benefit much from economic growth or tax reform. And so, if the Biblical prophesy were not to come to pass, a new approach to aiding the poor had to be found.

Thus was born what was known as the "income strategy." Since, by official definition, a person was poor because he lacked an adequate income, the simplest, more effective way to remove him from poverty would be to give him more money. As a practical matter, this meant expanding income support programs—both in coverage and in generosity—and adding new ones for those who were ineligible for any assistance. As a quick glance at budget figures from the mid-sixties onwards will show, this is, more or less, what occurred.

One consequence of this new approach was to change drastically the character of American social insurance and public assistance programs. Although alleviating poverty was never unimportant, the primary purpose of these programs was to provide a degree of financial security in the face of certain risks of modern life: retirement without adequate savings, death of a spouse, disability, unemployment, and divorce or desertion. As components of an "income strategy," however, they became vehicles for redistributing money from those who had it to those who did not. The result was to alter the moral basis of the entitlement; it was enough to be needy, no matter why or whether other means of support could be found.

Nonetheless, this seemed to be of little importance at first. What counted was that poverty seemed to be going down as social insurance and public assistance benefits went up. Though perhaps not as well as it could have if a more comprehensive measure like the Family Assistance Plan had been enacted, the "income strategy" still appeared to work, as more than veterans of the Great Society acknowledged. "The combination of strong economic growth and a dramatic increase in welfare and income transfer programs during the last decade has virtually wiped out poverty in the United States," wrote Martin Anderson in 1978. Even today, the "income strategy" continues to play a major role in reducing poverty; in 1984, perhaps as many as one-third of the poor left poverty not because of higher earnings but rather because of increased assistance from government.

However, there was another dimension to the "income strategy" that has gradually begun to loom larger. From the outset, the designers of this approach to eliminating poverty were mindful of the possibility that some number of people receiving benefits—particularly, but not only those capable of working—might be tempted to reduce their own efforts to obtain an adequate income. Hence, they initiated a series of controlled demonstrations—the "negative income tax experiments"—to see how important the problem might be. It turned out to be worth taking seriously indeed. Depending upon the characteristics of the income-support plan, large amounts of the money paid to the poor apparently replaced money that would otherwise have been earned. Furthermore, the availability of assistance seemed to increase the number of female-headed families, a group that was particularly likely to be impoverished. The implication of these results was that far from reducing poverty, pursuing an "income strategy" might make it worse.

That government has, in fact, done precisely that is, of course, the thesis of Charles Murray's *Losing Ground*. He argues that if poverty is measured on the basis of earned income alone, progress toward eliminating it stopped in the late 1960's, just as the "income strategy" was being introduced. And while many researchers have disputed this conclusion, it is consistent with other work, as well as a good deal of anecdotal evidence, such as that presented recently in a television report by Bill Moyers. If Murray and others are indeed correct, the price of "solving" the problem of poverty may have been an increase in the problem of welfare dependency.

Whether government is better at eliminating dependency than poverty is doubtful. So far, a variety of financial incentives, work-requirements, and other administrative controls have been tried, none to great effect. At best, workfare programs and child-support laws also seem of limited value. Cutting back on benefits, as Murray has hypothetically suggested (and as has actually occurred in many states in recent years), might succeed, but the price of an increased number of poor—at least in the short run—would probably have to be paid. Last year's statistics, for example, showed virtually no reduction in poverty among female-headed families with young children, much of whose income normally comes from welfare programs that have become less generous.

Thus, a dilemma. Government can eliminate poverty through an "income strategy," but doing so encourages more of the poor to rely on public assistance, instead of taking steps to become self-supporting. That, in turn, may sow the seeds of a deeper, more lasting poverty, which becomes more difficult to reduce, even with more generous benefits. If the poor need not always be with us, the dependent may be. And from society's point of view, that may not be a good bargain.

If there is a solution, perhaps the place to look is elsewhere than the income support programs. For the poor often lack not just money, but also the habits and skills, as well as the less tangible characteristics—like stable communities, supportive religious and kinship ties, and "middle-class" values—which traditionally have been essential for upward mobility. Government can foster some of these: indeed, more than it usually thinks. (For example, it would be worth examining whether welfare mothers who participate in workfare programs are more or less likely to remarry—the most common route out of poverty and dependency for these women—than those who do not.) It can also undermine them: indeed, more often than it usually thinks, as Nicholas Lemann shows so brilliantly in his essay in *The Atlantic*. If efforts to end poverty are not simply to wind up replacing it with dependency, public policy must tend to the impoverishment of the spirit as well as of the pocketbook.

LINKING PUBLIC AND PRIVATE EFFORTS IN OVERCOMING POVERTY

Glenn C. Loury

Some writers interested in American political culture often seem to argue that public debate over the poverty problem pits the selfish—who would cut programs, ignore need, leave the poor to fend for themselves—against the generous—who would redistribute income, expand programs and "care" about the indigent. Our public discourse on this issue is often couched in such terms; politicians are alternately judged "compassionate" or "callous," based on whether they favor respectively a greater or lesser role for the government in dealing with poverty. From this perspective the poverty debate becomes reduced to a dispute about what is the ethically correct distribution of "society's" income and wealth. Unfortunately, the poverty problem is not quite so simple as the demagogues would have you believe.

A standard method used by pundits to distinguish between liberals and conservatives is to ask people about their attitudes toward the poor. Conservatives, according to the conventional wisdom, think poverty is the result of individuals' failings of character. Liberals, in this view, see the poor as victims of societal failings—unemployment, racial discrimination. The view that poverty results from individual failings is seen by many as evidence of a lack of compassion; the notion that the poor are society's victims is often identified as a sign of concern for the indigent. At issue here is the empirical question concerning the extent to which changes in individuals' behavior can be expected to diminish the prevalence of poverty.

I submit that the question of the role of the private sector in eliminating poverty can be answered in part by reference to this conflict between liberal and conservative perceptions. My thesis is that, to the extent that poverty is linked to patterns of behavior among individuals which diminish their (and their children's) prospects of becoming productive, self-supporting members of society—to that extent, the role of private actions in the struggle against poverty becomes more important. Conversely, to the extent that poverty issues from societal failures—unfair discrimination, a depressed economy, inadequate educational preparation—the scope for private voluntary action to reduce it is limited. There is ample evidence to suggest that both individual and societal failures are at work in the contemporary American poverty problem.

Moreover, I suggest that the notions of "caring," or "compassion," or "progressive policy" or, even, "social justice" cannot be defined without reference to this judgment concerning the role played by individuals' behavior in generating poverty. It *is* indeed callous to say of someone whose children are starving because there is no work to be had—"Let him fend for himself." But is it compassionate to support policies which, though they provide money to indigent persons, also encourage those persons to act in ways that insure their permanent dependency? I think not.

The poverty population is not homogeneous. A great deal has been made of this fact in recent policy debate. Most persons who are below the poverty line at any point in time will be poor for a relatively short duration—no more than a year or two. Yet there also exists a minority of the poor who are likely to be virtually in permanent poverty. Indeed, it has been estimated that roughly one-half of AFDC payments are made to the less than one-quarter of recipients who are long-term dependents. This hard core, more or less permanently dependent population, is sometimes referred to as the "underclass." There is a large and growing body of data and evidence, both in the scholarly literature and the popular press, suggesting that the behavior and values of persons in this underclass—especially during their formative years of adolescence—play an important part in perpetuating their poverty. Problems such as early unwed pregnancy, alcohol and drug dependency, and chronic long-term joblessness are all, at least in part, a reflection of individuals' behavior and choices which make their impoverishment more likely. Addressing the poverty problem for this population means, ultimately, addressing the system of values and beliefs and the corresponding individual behaviors and actions which reduce a person's chance to become self-supporting.

Public policy certainly has a role to play in this—though I believe that it is the private, voluntary sector which must carry the main burden. Concerning the issue of individuals' poverty-inducing behaviors, I believe the main public policy consideration is to avoid rewarding "vice" (i.e., individual actions which retard their ability to become self-supporting—like having a child before being able to properly care for and support it), and to avoid punishing "virtue" (i.e., individual actions which promote independence). If a welfare mother must lose access to medical care for herself and her children when she takes a job, then public policy would seem to be punishing "virtue." If a rebellious teenager can, by having a child out of wedlock and becoming an "emancipated minor," secure the resources to establish her own household and live independently of her parents, then public policy would seem to be rewarding "vice."

Yet, the ability of public action to change the underlying values and preferences of poor persons—as distinct from changing the rewards associated with various individual choices—seems to be quite limited. It is extremely difficult for state and county welfare officials to win the "hearts and minds" of their clients, to alter their basic beliefs and aspirations, or to change substantively their behavior codes. Many such efforts have been undertaken—in the area of teen pregnancy, for example—with relatively little success.

On the other hand, we are increasingly learning about private, voluntary, community-based efforts which produce success in this area of changing the behavior of the poor. The Black Muslim movement, which flourished in many major American cities among inner-city blacks, provides but one example of this possibility. The work of community organizations such as that run by Ms. Kimi Gray at Kenilworth-Parkside in Washington, D.C. provides a current illustration of these possibilities. The home for unwed mothers in Lynchburg, Va., run by Rev. Falwell's church (in which there have been virtually *no* second unwed pregnancies among residents, despite the fact that nationally nearly one-half of teen unwed mothers have a second child out of wedlock) further illustrates what is being done. These are, borrowing the concept of Peter Berger and Richard John Neuhaus, "mediating structures"—social organizations smaller than government yet larger than the individual family, which operate among voluntary associations of individuals, and which are better able than governments to be effective at altering the basic behavior of their individual members.

It should not be surprising that churches, or residential associations, or civic groups are potentially more effective at changing the underlying values and behaviors of their individual members than the bureaucratic alternative. Mutually concerned persons who trust one another enough to be able to exchange criticism constructively, establish codes of personal conduct, and enforce social sanctions against what is judged as undesirable behavior, can create and enforce communal norms that lie beyond the capacity of the state to effectively promulgate. The coercive resources of the state, though great, are not especially subtle. Yet within voluntary associations of individuals, precisely because they are voluntary and operate with the consent of those concerned, powerful mechanisms of persuasion are available. The threat of social ostracism—of the withdrawal from the individual of approval and respect by those whose high regard is most avidly sought—can encourage individuals to conform to the expectations and opinions of "significant others" in ways that the threat of incarceration cannot.

Thus, to the extent that reducing poverty requires changing the behavior of persons at high risk of becoming poor (e.g., avoidance of early unwed pregnancy, maintenance of steady employment in a low-wage job while gaining work experience and a stable employment record)—to that extent, the public sector faces basic disadvantages in effecting such "changes of preference." For encouraging "virtuous" behavior intrinsically requires judgments about and discriminations among people that are difficult (legally, politically) for public agencies to make. It seems that only persons close enough to the situation can have the standing to be able to effectively make and enforce such judgments.

This is particularly so when such distinctions are likely to have disparate impacts by race. For example, school districts with racially disproportionate student suspension rates have had to face racial discrimination charges, and investigation by the Office of Civil Rights of the Department of Education. And yet, as the celebrated and very successful Paterson, N.J., principal Joe Clark has shown, the *judicious* use of suspensions and expulsions in inner-city schools can be a very effective tool for improving the educational environment.

When it comes to reaching and changing the values of black youngsters in today's big-city ghettos, the example of Ms. Gray at Kenilworth-Parkside convincingly illustrates that the power of private, voluntary associations must be harnessed if long-term poverty is to be significantly reduced in such populations.

We should note that for many a discussion of public and private responsibilities in the struggle against poverty is a discussion about the appropriate distribution of income, a discourse in the field of social justice. I have suggested here that such a view of the problem is too limited to usefully guide this important debate. We, of course, must engage in political debate about the extent of obligation which the well-off among us have to those less fortunate. But the problem of poverty is not simply equivalent to an absence of money among certain household heads. And finding the right public policies to deal with this problem requires more from us than determination of our mutual obligations.

Finally, to the extent that long-term poverty reflects behavior (e.g., unwed child-bearing among adolescents) which can be modified only by changing persons' basic values and aspirations, such transformation must take place primarily within the private sector. No degree of mutual social obligation, enforced through the taxation and transfer policies of the state, can substitute for what is to be had within freely entered associations of individuals. For these latter can establish and enforce for their members communal norms that work to reduce the prevalence of poverty-inducing behaviors.

FAMILY, WORK, AND WELFARE REFORM

Carl A. Anderson

When President Kennedy sent to Congress his welfare message of 1962—a message which would lay the foundation of the Great Society program that would soon follow—he defined the criteria by which its success would be measured. He stated that public welfare programs should strengthen the family, reduce divorce and illegitimacy, and enhance employment. In the past two decades substantial independent research has measured just how successful these income transfer programs have been in improving the economic and family life of poor Americans.

One of the most important studies of the success of cash benefit programs in reducing poverty was undertaken by Sheldon Danziger and Robert Plotnick.[1] Their research found that $12.6 billion (in 1983 dollars) of cash transfer payments in 1967 reduced poverty 0.7 percentage points. By 1974, such cash transfer payments had risen to $26.6 billion (again in 1983 dollars) but had resulted in only a 1.0 percentage reduction.

Thus, from zero to $12.6 billion in cash payments, the marginal reduction in the poverty rate per billion dollars was one-half of one percent (.056). But from $12.6 billion to $26.6 billion in transfers the marginal reduction in the poverty rate was only a surprising two-tenths of one percent (.021) for each billion dollars of payments. Danziger and Plotnick conclude that while a certain level of cash benefits may reduce poverty, increasing benefits beyond a certain level may actually have a negative impact on the rate of poverty reduction. They observe that cash payments have reached such proportions that the accompanying work disincentive actually leads to higher rates of poverty.

This research is consistent with the earlier Seattle-Denver Income Maintenance Experiments in which poor families in both cities were studied over a ten-year period.[2] Control groups were given a cash benefit of 115 percent of the poverty line. The study found that for every $100 provided to male-headed families, earnings fell by $25 to $50 and for female-headed families earnings fell at even a greater rate. The results of the Seattle-Denver study strongly suggest why it is that by 1984, only 7.2 percent of poor mothers who were also the head of their households worked full time.

This Poverty-Welfare Curve, in which crossing a threshold of increasing welfare benefits corresponds with an increase in poverty, is consistent with the behavior of the poverty rate. From the beginning of the War on Poverty in the 1960s through 1973, the poverty rate in the United States consistently declined until it reached 11 percent. Since that time it has just as consistently increased until it reached a post-1965 high of more than fifteen percent in 1983.[3]

One tremendously important factor involved in the reversal of this trend was the 1968 decision of the United States Supreme Court to strike down the welfare eligibility rule of many States prohibiting a "substitute father" from living in the home of an unmarried welfare mother.[4] By mandating cash benefits under the Aid to Families with Dependent Children program to unmarried mothers in households in which a "substitute father" was present, the Supreme Court redirected our national welfare system to provide a substantial incentive for the break-up of poor families.

The Bureau of the Census indicates that families headed by never-married and formerly-married women account for forty-seven percent of the 7.6 million families with incomes below the poverty level.[5] Research cited by the United States Civil Rights Commission in its report entitled, *A Growing Crisis: Disadvantaged Women and Their Children,* suggests that increasing divorce and the extraordinary rise in unwed motherhood "are responsible for essentially all of the growth in poverty since 1970."[6]

The Seattle-Denver study found a significant rise in divorce associated with large cash payments to families in which both husband and wife were present. The problem is that large cash payments undercut the husband's economic role within the family. The trap for intact families which large benefits create is that, although the benefits begin while the husband is present, they continue to the wife and children following divorce. In addition, the economies of scale within marriage may be compensated for upon divorce by other governmental benefits related to housing, food, health care, and energy costs. Thus, the same financial incentives accompanying large welfare benefits which affect a woman's decision to begin a family outside marriage may also influence her decision to discontinue a marriage. Especially is this true when these financial incentives are accompanied by the Supreme Court's insistence that benefits continue when a "substitute father" is present.

High cash benefits provide a substantial financial incentive to go on welfare and once there, to stay on welfare. In a new study prepared for the Joint Economic Committee of Congress, Ohio University professors Lowell Gallaway and Richard Vedder found that until a poverty child reaches the age of twelve, welfare benefits actually exceed the marginal costs of raising the child; and by the time the child reaches the age of seventeen years, those benefits will exceed the cost of raising him by $3,000.[7] The problem is that welfare benefits can provide more actual income than many entry-level jobs. For example, in a high benefit state, welfare programs can provide a family of three with combined benefits of approximately $14,000. But to enjoy the same living standard without welfare, that family would have to earn at least $18,000.[8]

The results of these financial incentives can be seen in the child poverty rates among the states. Between 1969 and 1979, the fifteen states with the highest cash benefit levels experienced a twenty-six percent increase in child poverty while the fifteen states with the lowest levels of AFDC payments experienced an average *decrease* in child poverty of nearly fifteen percent. This difference remains even after controlling for differing economic conditions among the states.[9] Gallaway and Vedder found that if a high AFDC benefit state, such as New York, had in 1977 adopted the benefit level of a low benefit state like Texas, by 1980, New York would have had 159,000 *fewer* female-headed families in poverty.[10]

These trends have proven devastating to millions of America's children. While the poverty rate for children generally exceeds the overall poverty rate, the relationship between the two rates has shifted dramatically during the last three decades. In 1959, for example, the child poverty rate was 4.5 percentage points greater than the overall rate. By 1969, that difference had fallen to only 1.7 percent. But by the next year that trend had reversed and the difference continued to widen until it stood at 6.6 percent in 1984.[11]

Gallaway and Vedder conclude "that poverty among children was over twenty percent greater than it would have been in the absence of the massive post-1969 growth in the number and size of federal programs." If correct, that translates into 2.5 million more children in poverty because of increases in public assistance.[12] Today, welfare has become the invisible husband and father for millions of poor families.

The findings we have been discussing do not suggest that we should abandon the poor—far from it. But they do suggest that the problem of poverty in America is not going to be solved by throwing money at it. This challenge requires the courage to confront a problem which many welfare analysts think makes true welfare reform impossible. Their pessimism stems from the interaction between high marginal tax rates on the low-income worker and the benefit reduction formulas in high benefit welfare programs that cause benefits to be reduced relative to the amount of earned income.

Some economists describe this relationship between earned income and reduced benefits as a marginal tax. When they do so, they can point to rates of this so-called marginal tax as high as—80, 85, and 90 percent. When benefit reductions are combined with steeply progressive tax rates for low-income taxpayers, a poverty wall is created which destroys the incentive to leave welfare and seek employment.

But to conclude, as many Washington experts have done, that this poverty wall makes welfare reform impossible overlooks two basic considerations. First, it is misleading to talk about benefit reduction as a tax, since it equates welfare benefits with the earned income of taxpayers. We are not talking here about children, the elderly, or the disabled. We are talking about able-bodied people without young children, and these people really should not be given the option of refusing employment in order to stay on welfare. Second, we need to remember that a welfare recipient's first job is just that—a first job. It is the first step up the economic ladder to a better financial future.

During his first term, President Reagan provided that better financial future for millions of Americans. In 1985, we witnessed:

- the largest reduction in the rate of poverty since 1968 with 1.8 million Americans lifted out of poverty;
- child poverty down in the largest decline since 1976;
- poverty among persons in female-headed households down in the largest decline since 1966;
- poverty among black Americans down in the largest decline since 1973;
- poverty among the elderly down for the fourth straight year in a row to an all time low.

The past fifty months have been nearly thirteen million new jobs created. One out of every six of these new jobs went to a black American. President Reagan's tremendous success in moving millions of Americans out of poverty is in large measure due to his insistence that welfare programs can be reformed and the poverty wall broken down.

In 1981, the Omnibus Budget Reconciliation Act for the first time permitted states to require able-bodied welfare recipients who do not have young children to participate in Community Work Experience Programs. Under this approach welfare agencies assign AFDC recipients to work in public or private non-profit agencies. Recipients provide public service and acquire work experience in exchange for their benefits. Today, thirty-nine states have implemented some form of an innovative work experience program.

These job experience programs provide not only training and new skills but something far more basic: motivation and self-confidence. For example, one twenty-six year old participant explained that she had been on AFDC since she was seventeen years old. She had never been employed, and she did not think that she had anything to offer an employer. Through a community work experience program, she had been put to work in a clerical position in a state office. In four months, she had learned to type, to file, and to answer the telephones. She said, "I never thought I could even get up every day and catch a bus, much less get up every day, catch a bus and go to work. Now I know that if no one showed up in this office tomorrow, I could run it all by myself for the day."

In 1982, we were able to enact legislation to permit, for the first time, states to require job search by AFDC applicants and recipients. Under these programs, state agencies help individuals prepare for and find employment by providing help with identifying jobs, job interviewing and completing job applications.

In 1985, the State of California passed, with broad bi-partisan support, comprehensive legislation to establish a statewide work experience program with an estimated savings of $100 million annually. The money is important, but far more important is the new independence to be gained for thousands of low-income families.

A recent Government Accounting Office survey of 55 state work experience programs found that 270,545 welfare participants obtained gainful employment in 1985. Only one-quarter of these programs placed fewer than twenty percent of their participants in jobs.[13]

The President has also moved to break down the poverty wall from the earned income side by restoring employment incentives. His historic tax reforms of 1981 and of 1986 greatly lowered the high marginal tax rates paid by low-income working families. Equally important, the President's 1986 tax reform exempts families below the poverty level from paying federal income tax. For example, last year a family of four started paying tax when its income exceeded $9,575—approximately $1,825 below the poverty line.[14] By adding such an additional burden to poor families, the old tax system was a substantial barrier to their climbing out of poverty. Thanks to President Reagan that is no longer the case.

Domestic policy need not be a zero-sum game in a society of scarce resources and diminishing growth. The first six years of the Reagan Administration demonstrated that the poor can be lifted up from dependency without impoverishing those better off. To help the less fortunate is one of our country's noblest endeavors. To abandon the poor would be to demean ourselves; but to help the poor without giving them a real chance to escape poverty is to degrade us all. We can provide the escape from poverty by building an economy which creates more jobs. We can empower people so that, as President Reagan has said, even "the least among us shall have an equal chance to achieve the greatest things."

NOTES

[1]*Children in Poverty,* Committee Print, Committee on Ways and Means, U.S. House of Representatives (Washington, D.C., 1985), pp. 157-58.

[2]Aaron, Henry Jr., Six Welfare Questions Still Searching for Answers, The Brookings Review (Fall, 1984) pp. 13-14.

[3]*Poverty, Income Distribution, the Family and Public Policy,* Joint Committee Print, Joint Economic Committee, U.S. Congress (Washington, D.C., 1986) p. 34.

[4]*King v. Smith,* 392 U.S. 309 (1968).

[5]U.S. Bureau of the Census, *Current Population Reports: Consumer Income* (series P-60, No. 145, 1984) p. 4.

[6]U.S. Commission on Civil Rights, *A Growing Crisis: Disadvantaged Women and Their Children* (1983) p. 62.

[7]*Supra* note 3 at p. 61.

[8]*Up From Dependency: A New National Public Assistance Strategy,* A Report to the President by the Domestic Policy Council Low Income Opportunity Working Group (December, 1986) p. 26.

[9]*Supra* note 3 at p. 59.

[10]*Id.,* at p. 83.

[11]*Id.,* at p. 56.

[12]*Id.,* at p. 62.

[13]U.S. General Accounting Office, *Work and Welfare: Current AFDC Work Programs and Implications for Federal Policy* (Washington D.C., 1987) p. 100.

[14]*The President's Tax Proposals to the Congress for Fairness, Growth, and Simplicity* (U.S. Government Printing Office, 1985), p. 6.

A NEW FOCUS FOR WELFARE

Blanche Bernstein

Analysis of the profile of poverty in 1984 leads me to divide the poor into two groups: one which will benefit from an improvement in the general level of the economy, a reduction in unemployment, some tax changes, or some relatively modest changes in the social insurance and welfare programs; the other, in the main, will not benefit from such developments. Rather, for this group, we must seek a change in social behavior. The first group includes the elderly, intact families with children under 18 years of age or only older children. The second group includes female-headed families with children under 18 as well as the smaller number of such male headed families, and unrelated individuals, especially those 18 to 25 years old.

It is important to focus on the female-headed family with children under 18 and the unrelated individuals 18-25. They suffer the highest rates of poverty. Female-headed families with young children are 8.5 percent of the population but constitute 31 percent of all persons in poverty; 53 percent of all such families are poor. The 18-25 year old group of individuals are 2 percent of the population and 4 percent of the poor; about a third of these young singles are poor. I put them together because it appears that many of these young people come from AFDC families, are school drop-outs, and are having great difficulties breaking into the labor market. These two groups are the long term poor and most receive AFDC or general assistance. Their lot did not improve much as a result of the decline in poverty from 1983 to 1984. They will not gain much from increased tax allowances for dependents. Nor in my view will welfare reform permitting additional incentives to work or fine tuning of marginal tax rates make any difference. Finally, we cannot reduce poverty for this group either by substantially increasing welfare allowances or by abolishing the welfare system altogether in the hope that adversity will somehow strengthen character. Neither one nor the other will be acceptable to the American people.

The current and long overdue emphasis on a work obligation for the heads of families on welfare, the provisions for job search, skills training and workfare will make some difference and must be pursued vigorously. But it has its limitations. It has to be recognized as a salvage operation. The welfare mothers will be starting late on working careers. Their education is likely to be limited to high school graduation or the equivalent and their earnings are likely to be modest. Some may still require welfare supplementation, others may have earnings not much above the poverty level.

What then? We should try to change social behavior, particularly to prevent teenage pregnancy, dropping out of school and promote family stability. These are the major causes of long term poverty. Teenage pregnancy has been receiving a lot of attention in the last few years. A variety of programs are now in place but mainly these are designed to help the pregnant teenager or teenage mother, when the first priority ought to be to prevent the first pregnancy. The federal government in cooperation with state and local governments, national and local voluntary organizations should provide subsidized additional resources to the effort to prevent teenage pregnancy.

With respect to education—the policy decisions of the 60s and early 70s to open the public colleges to every high school graduate who chose to go has achieved only modest success and at a very substantial cost in remediation efforts. We must begin much earlier—with the four year old in pre-kindergarten and continue with special programs till the child is twelve and within grade for reading, writing, and math. We cannot say to the child of six, you have had a headstart, now sink or swim in the educational pool. Too many will sink.

If we are to break the cycle of dependency and poverty, it is the children of the welfare mothers who need attention and the bulk of the services which can be made available from added resources. One of the utter failures of the welfare system is that it has done little, if anything, to improve the care and upbringing of the children on welfare, leaving this task exclusively to the mother, predominantly the teenage mother, or a teenager when her first child was born, in complete disregard of her obvious limitations for the task. For the most part, only in cases of disaster—child abuse or neglect—does the local welfare department intervene.

The philosophy of non-intervention developed in the 1960s as part of the notion that any and all life styles were acceptable. The attitude then was that there is nothing wrong with the welfare family that a little more money wouldn't cure, and the victims should not be blamed for the plight. It was the system that was to blame. Twenty years later, we have sufficient evidence to prove that without early intervention, the welfare family's situation is likely to get worse, not better.

Welfare departments, however, have become so engrossed in simply running the income maintenance and Medicaid system more effectively and dealing with the disasters represented by the need for foster placement of children, shelter for the homeless, or child abuse in day care centers, that they have forgotten how to help a family get its act together. Welfare staff should be helping mothers learn how to care for their infants and toddlers properly in terms of nutrition and health care and how to instill in their children the habits and values which will propel them to a better preparation for their adolescent and adult lives.

There are experts in these matters who can be brought on to welfare staffs to organize the appropriate group sessions. Attendance should be compulsory for the welfare mothers, and for the adolescent boys and girls, on pain of reductions in the welfare grant for absence without cause. Only through some such effort can the welfare system, working with the schools and with appropriate voluntary agencies make a real and lasting contribution to the reduction of poverty. This is the major welfare reform which I would promote.

Let me also express the hope that in a society which places such high value on the family that we will soon eliminate a perverse aspect of the federal welfare system, one which discriminates against the intact family. It does not make adequate provision for cash assistance to such families where incomes are below the poverty level even when the wage earner is employed.

While the federally supported AFDC program is available to the family with an unemployed parent or one who is working less than 100 hours per month, only twenty-six states have chosen to establish such programs and somewhat fewer assist the family with a fully employed parent earning an income below the welfare standard. In the remaining states, no welfare assistance (except for food stamps) is available to intact families no matter how low their income.

Legislation to remedy this omission was again introduced in the 1985-86 session of the Congress, but it was deleted in the March version of the budget. Efforts are now being made by some members of the Congress to restore it. Its passage would not only remove the current inequity but it might to some degree prevent family break-up, especially in periods of economic distress.

HARD CHOICES: BALANCING VALUES IN WELFARE POLICY

June O'Neill

Headlines citing "Hunger in America" have appeared frequently in recent years. So have reports of rising spending on public transfer programs. Although the stories of need have been linked to stories of welfare spending, different analysts have reached quite opposite conclusions. While some maintain that welfare spending has not been adequate to address the problem, others claim that the rise in poverty is the result of too much spending on welfare. This essay will address the factors underlying changes in poverty and the effects of welfare on poverty and on dependency.

Poverty and the Economy

Between 1973 and 1983 the poverty rate rose from 11.1 percent to 15.3 percent. The real income of the average American male was almost 20 percent lower in 1983 than in 1973; so it should come as no surprise that the income of those at the lowest portion of the income distribution also fell, resulting in a rise in poverty.

The relation between the economy and poverty is a long-standing one. It was basically the remarkably high rate of economic growth that caused the poverty rate to decline by close to two-thirds over the post World War II period. Economic stagnation set in during the 1970s and poverty rose with the series of recessions of the 70s and early 80s.

Poverty and Transfers

In principle it should be possible for policy to directly affect the number of people in poverty, regardless of the state of the economy, by taxing the rich and giving to the poor. This seemingly simple solution has no doubt motivated government transfer policy towards the poor. Broadly defined, publicly funded social welfare expenditure increased from 11 percent to 19 percent of GNP over the period 1965 to 1983.

There are several reasons why this dramatic change in the transfer system would not reduce poverty to the extent one might expect. One reason is that a large share of these transfers was not directed exclusively at poor people. The social insurance programs (including social security, medicare, public retirement, and unemployment compensation) make up more than half of all social welfare expenditures. These programs are intended to replace a significant fraction of income during retirement or unemployment. While poor individuals also benefit, the largest benefits go to those with higher incomes.

However, although social security was an inefficient way to reduce poverty among the elderly, it was sufficiently massive to have contributed to a significant reduction in poverty for this particular group. (The poverty rate for persons 65 and older declined from 25 percent in 1969 to 14 percent in 1979, while the rate for all persons rose by three percentage points.)

Another reason why transfers have not had a greater effect on the overall poverty rate is that a growing share of all transfers is given in the form of noncash benefits, which are not counted as income for the purpose of measuring the official poverty rate. (These benefits include food stamps, medicare, medicaid and housing subsidies.) The Census Bureau, however, now provides estimates of the poverty rate based on a definition of income that includes an estimated value of noncash benefits. In 1984, this adjusted poverty rate (in which noncash benefits were measured by their market value) was 9.7 percent compared to the unadjusted "official" rate of 14.4 percent.

A third and more substantive reason why transfers do not reduce poverty as much as expected is that the transfers themselves have offsetting effects. A dollar of benefits does not simply add a dollar to a needy individual's income since it creates incentives for individuals to change their behavior in order to qualify. For example, as social security benefits rose in value, the labor force participation of older men fell sharply (from 47 percent in 1948 to 16 percent in 1984, for those 65 and over). And as disability benefits were expanded, a larger proportion of the population stopped working for reasons of disability. To estimate the true poverty-reducing effect of social security or other transfers requires that we know the magnitude of the work disincentive effect, a difficult problem to solve.

Welfare Programs

The subset of programs that are means tested—that is, they are restricted to those with low incomes—make up a minor share of all transfer programs. Nonetheless, these programs have grown over time and are by no means insignificant. (Such programs include Aid to Families with Dependent Children, (AFDC); Supplemental Security Income, (SSI); and Food Stamps, Medicaid, and child nutrition programs.) In 1983 they amounted to $103 billion (in 1984 dollars) about four times the amount spent in 1965 in real terms (Table 1). As a percentage of GNP they rose from 1 percent in 1965 to about 3 percent in 1975 and have remained at the 3 percent level.

The effects of these transfers on poverty is particularly difficult to measure, in part because these transfers are increasingly in the form of non-cash benefits (close to 75 percent in 1984), and in part because the disincentives are complex.

The program most closely identified with welfare—Aid to Families with Dependent Children (AFDC)—is a case in point.

TABLE 1
Means Tested Public Welfare Expenditures
(in Billions of 1984 $)

Fiscal Year	Cash Benefits[1]	In-Kind Benefits[2]	Total	Total as % of GNP
1960	12.4	5.1	17.5	1.0
1965	14.8	10.6	25.4	1.1
1970	24.7	27.7	52.4	1.0
1975	33.4	56.2	89.6	2.9
1979	31.1	75.3	106.4	3.0
1981	29.7	76.4	106.1	3.1
1983	29.8	73.0	102.8	3.0

[1]Categorical cash payment programs including Aid to Families with Dependent Children, Supplemental Security Income, and general assistance.

[2]Includes medicaid, food stamps, maternal and child health programs, child nutrition programs, other food programs, low-income energy assistance program, and other certain social service and work-experience programs.

Source: Social Security Bulletin, February 1986.

More than one kind of disincentive may operate—one, the usual work disincentive; another, a disincentive to marry or remarry.

The pattern of growth in the AFDC caseload over time corresponds closely to the change in the benefit level provided. Between 1963 and 1972 the average real benefit (for a family of four with no other income) increased by 35 percent. This does not reflect the introduction of Medicaid or of public housing, school meals or other programs and services, which significantly added to the value of the welfare package. Even without these add-ons the cash benefits plus food stamps provided an average allotment of close to $9000 in 1972 (for the family of four without other income, expressed in 1984 dollars). This income was tax free and required no hours of work away from home or work expenses. It may well have appeared an attractive alternative for a woman with little education or few work skills and with poor marriage prospects.

Between 1963 and 1972, the period of rapid benefit increase, the number of female headed families on AFDC tripled. This was the result of a doubling in the percentage of female headed families going on the program (from 33 percent to 67 percent) as well as a 50 percent rise in the number of female headed families.

After 1976, the total AFDC benefit package began to erode as states failed to raise AFDC cash benefit levels to keep pace with inflation. At that point, the AFDC caseload stopped rising. Following the changes introduced in the Omnibus Budget Reconciliation Act of 1981, which deliberalized benefits somewhat, there was a decline in the caseload, despite rising unemployment which usually causes a cyclical increase.

The data strongly suggest that rising welfare benefit levels are associated with an increase in welfare participation. Studies that control for other factors have also demonstrated this relation. This is a matter of concern because of the strong possibility that welfare participation affects behavior by discouraging work or marriage. The sharper rise and higher level of marital dissolution among blacks is hard to explain in any other way. (Between 1960 and 1983 the proportion of families headed by a woman rose from 8 percent to 12 percent for whites and from 22 percent to 42 percent for blacks.)

Differences between the North and the South in the share of families headed by women may also be traced to differences in welfare levels. In the South, the maximum AFDC benefit for a family of four ranges from $120 to $379 a month, while outside the South the benefit ranges from $282 to $676 a month. Despite lower levels of schooling in the South, a characteristic associated with out-of-wedlock births and marital dissolution, the percentage of black families headed by women was 40 percent in the South compared to 48 percent outside the South. (Among black children, 46 percent were in female headed families in the South; 59 percent outside the South). Among white families, 12 percent in the South and 13 percent in the non-South were female headed. These data suggest, although they do not prove, that welfare benefit levels may have had important behavioral effects. It is also noteworthy that the low benefit strategy of the South has not produced more poverty. Quite the contrary, the measured poverty rate in 1984 among female headed families was somewhat lower for both blacks and whites in the South than it was in the high benefit North and West. Evidently, women in the South, who are less likely to be on welfare, develop more work experience and have higher earnings, which more than compensates for the lower benefits.

TABLE 2
Trends in AFDC Families and Benefits and in
Female Headed Families with Children

	Number of AFDC Families[1]	Number of Female Headed Families with Children (FHFC)	Annual AFDC Families as Percent of FHFC	Real AFDC & Food Stamp Benefit (1984's)[2]	Benefits as Percent of:[3]	
					Male Annual Earnings	Female Annual Earning (Full-Time Year-Round Workers)
1964	992	2895	34.3	6604	42.4	53.2
1968	1400	3269	42.8	7129	39.9	52.3
1972	2915	4322	76.4	8894	48.1	59.2
1976	3444	5310	64.8	8743	50.8	57.6
1980	3570	6299	56.6	7486	47.4	51.2
1984	3438	6832	50.3	6955	44.6	45.1

[1]Excludes families with an unemployed father. Average monthly number of recipients in calendar year except for 1984 which is for the fiscal year.
[2]Benefits for a family of four with no other income.
[3]AFDC and food stamp benefit as measured in column 4.

Source: AFDC families: Social Security Bulletin, various issues.
Female headed families with Children: Committee on Ways and Means (1985b).
AFDC and food stamp benefit levels: Committee on Ways and Means (1985a), p. 532.
Annual earnings (median): Council of Economic Advisers (1986), Table B-29.

Perhaps the most important question about the effects of AFDC concerns the effects long-term welfare dependency has on the children in AFDC families. Are they more likely to become unemployed, to commit crimes, to be less well motivated in school, to become teenage mothers and ultimately to go on welfare? Because of a lack of data, solid research in these areas is lacking, although abundant anecdotal evidence suggests that these outcomes may be real.

Conclusion

The extent of poverty in the nation has largely been determined by the state of the economy. Efforts to redistribute income have succeeded in shifting income from the young to the old; and at enormous cost have helped to reduce poverty among the aged. Transfers from the rich to the poor among the nonelderly population have been done on a more modest scale, but with little observable positive effects on measured incomes.

It is difficult if not impossible, however, to design a system intended to provide assistance to needy families headed by an able bodied adult and at the same time avoid harmful disincentives. "Need" is not an inherent trait but is to a large extent the consequence of voluntary decisions relating to work, fertility, and marriage. Therefore, the extent of need is not a fixed number, but is susceptible to change based on incentives offered. Efforts to change behavior through work requirements and work and training programs have not had significant effects as the history of the WIN program testifies. If welfare benefits remain high, work programs will always have trouble competing. On the other hand, individuals can become the victims of past choices, and particularly where children are concerned it is difficult to ignore their plight. These conflicts have created the basic dilemma of welfare.

Hard choices must, therefore, be made. Implicitly, the public has chosen to cut back on welfare. The level of funding provided to welfare programs has leveled off in the past decade. Cash benefit levels in AFDC have declined in real terms. As a result, the welfare caseload has also stopped rising. There also are signs that the formation of female headed families is not rising as rapidly as it was, and that the out-of-wedlock birth rate is steady or falling slightly.

In seeking new welfare options, one possible direction is to remove the open-ended aspect of AFDC for families headed by able bodied adults and to place a finite limit on program duration, as is the case with unemployment insurance. In this way welfare would no longer be able to replace other sources of income on a permanent basis. Another direction already underway is the requirement that absent fathers contribute to their children's support. Although the income provided might not remove many from the AFDC caseload, it would perhaps foster greater concern for the consequences of behavior and, hence, prevent the birth of chidren who cannot be supported by their parents. Finally, it should be emphasized that preventive measures, such as improving basic education, may have the added pay-off of reducing welfare dependency in the long run.

STATE AND LOCAL GOVERNMENT PROGRAM DESIGN AND ADMINISTRATION—THE ONLY TRUE WELFARE REFORM

Robert B. Carleson

My views on welfare, poverty and possible solutions are based on experience. As a city manager or assistant for twelve years; Director of the California State Department of Social Welfare during Ronald Reagan's welfare reform of 1971-3; U.S. Commissioner on Welfare from 1973-5 and later as a consultant to a Member of Congress, governors and local officials, I have concluded that welfare reform based on income redistribution principles and national standards would be harmful to the poor and disastrous to the nation. On the other hand, a system based on work for the able and state or local government *designed* and administered assistance tailored to the individual family is the only true welfare reform. The alternative is simply an efficient system for redistributing income.

When I was director of welfare for the state of California in 1971-2, the conventional wisdom was that the states could not handle welfare. I remember they laughed at us because we thought that we could significantly reform welfare in California. At that time, the Nixon Family Assistance Plan was in the Senate Finance Committee and again the conventional wisdom was that states could not bring welfare under control. Because of this argument many people who ordinarily do not support nationalizing welfare were reluctantly supporting the Nixon Administration Plan.

When we in California completed our welfare reform, we found that we had in effect reduced benefits to people who were in the upper-income levels of the welfare group and increased the benefits to those in the lower levels, and found that the conventional wisdom failed again. The expectation was that those people who had a reduction in benefits or who were removed from the rolls entirely would simply leave their jobs and come back on the welfare rolls. As a matter of fact, the opposite occurred.

Of course this phenomenon was really not reported much in the East (apparently it was not reported in California either, in fairness), but was only generally reported as being controversial. When we did these same things at the national level, in 1981, President Reagan's first year in office, the welfare reforms in the budget were patterned largely on the California experience. The experts again predicted that when benefits are reduced or eliminated for people who are working and who are on welfare, the result would be that they would quit working and return to the welfare rolls. The studies since that time have proven very definitely that this did not happen at all.

One of our principal conclusions is that the welfare system can be tightened. And we can actually eliminate dependency on welfare for a very significant number of people, which is a very important finding. Another discovery we made along the way was that there are two versions of welfare reform. One version was a true welfare reform of developing an effective system to meet the basic needs of people who through no fault of their own require some kind of government assistance. And there was a welfare reform which was really nothing more than an income redistribution program, where the goal is simply to move money from those people who have it and have earned it and give it to other people. Such a system for the redistribution of income would require a national program with benefit levels set nationally, even if the amount is not any more than a minimum and for which eligibility is determined on income rather than on other factors such as disability or any other of the categorical factors, and where the benefits are in the form of cash. Such a system would immediately become subject to political pressures, and the minimum benefits would be increased further and further, notwithstanding whether or not people were truly in need.

Real assistance to the truly needy, to those who have to depend on the government in some way, is just the opposite, and cannot be, in my opinion, a national, centralized system in which computers can spew out checks in a very generalized manner and where eligibility is very roughly determined based on somebody's income record. To assist the needy only, and truly have a welfare system based on the precepts I have indicated requires that all benefit levels and eligibility requirements as well as administration be delegated to the lowest level of government possible.

Under our system in this country, from the federal point of view, this means delegation to the state government. When I was in the California state government, we concluded it was important to delegate as much of that as we could to the next level of government, which were the counties within the state. I strongly believe that a real solution to the welfare problem or poverty problem will be found by moving this authority and a certain amount of responsibility to the state and local levels of the government.

Another important consideration is that the general public as well as leading academics have concluded that able bodied persons should earn their welfare benefits. We found in California and later nationally, that "Workfare" works, but only when designed and administered at the State or local level.

A perennial question posed at this point is that the states seem "to be hard up for money" and "can they afford this program being dumped on them?" From the design and the policy point of view, we have not stated that there would be no funds. My preference, and solution at least for the time being and probably for a much longer period, would be simply to redirect the monies for the various programs that often overlap and duplicate each other into what some would call a block grant. By this or any other name, it is the finite amount of money that would be given to the state to be used only for assistance for those who are in need and with only a few strings attached. There would be no provisions for any national minimum benefit program which could get out of hand.

Only this kind of a process will solve the problem of poverty and welfare. It is pleasing to note that shift occurring which will make this solution possible. Jonathan Yardley of *The Washington Post* reviewed Lawrence Mead's new book "Beyond Entitlement", and it seems it is now *fashionable* to believe that welfare, "free-money" so to speak, causes the tendency for undesirable consequences, and calls for some mechanisms developed to earn the benefits provided. Another recent article in *The Washington Post* by William Raspberry relates his remedy of the problem through the discovery of a obscure Tocqueville piece on the fact that public welfare which he called "public charity" perpetuates idleness on the majority of the poor and provides for their leisure at the expense of those who worked. Finally, a quote from a 1978 conference continues to impress me. It concerns the perversity of our welfare system: "We go to a young girl, who's now 18 or 16 or even younger and this is what we say, 'abandon all of your hopes, your schools will not teach you, you will not learn to read or write, you will never have a decent job, you will live in the neighborhoods of endless unemployment and poverty with drugs and violence', but then we say to this child, 'wait, there is a way, one way, you can be somebody to someone, that will give you an apartment and furniture to fill it; we will give you a T.V. set and telephone, we will give you clothing and cheap food and free medical care and some spending money besides, and in turn you only have to do one thing, that is go out there and have a baby.'' The man who said that was Edward Kennedy in an address before the annual conference of the Michigan NAACP in Detroit. When this was first read to me, my guesses were that the author was almost anyone other than Edward Kennedy, particularly in 1978.

The years of discussion of welfare have brought about general agreement on some matters. One is that welfare can cause dependency. Secondly, that dependency is bad and it hurts people. We are also moving toward consensus on the point that people who are able should be expected to earn their basic benefits or any other kinds of benefits. I notice that people who have changed their position over the years will frequently still accuse those of us who held those positions for all those years of having the wrong reasons, the wrong motives. But I can assure you that President Reagan, when he was Governor and I was welfare director in the state of California, felt at that time, that people who need not be on welfare should not be made dependent for their own good.

Conclusion

I have concluded that the only solution will be to move these programs to the state and local levels of government. If necessary, the federal government should finance the programs through some kind of block grant particularly as it would relate to redistributing money among the states, not the individuals. States that are more poor should receive a significant amount more than the other states. Through this, and with the states imposing a requirement that welfare benefits will not be given unless they are earned in some way, by working or by going to school or both, can we ameliorate and someday significantly reduce poverty. More importantly, it will reduce dependency because those who are earning their way are certainly from an emotional standpoint able to break out of the cycle and get that second job and that third job, and move up the ladder of progress and independence, which is the ultimate goal.

CHILD SUPPORT ENFORCEMENT AND WELFARE REFORM

James S. Denton

The need for an efficient child support enforcement system demands our attention. The dramatic increase in the number of children denied financial support by their parents and the corresponding growth in social welfare spending has stimulated renewed interest in enforcement of parental responsibility. The Congress established the Child Support Enforcement (CSE) program in 1975 as part of the Social Security Act, and passed the Child Support Enforcement Amendments of 1984 to further the goals of the program. States now have greater incentives to secure financial support from absent parents—almost always fathers—for their children. If the amount of child support collected through the program is large enough, the family can be lifted out of welfare dependency. The program holds the promise of preventing dependency as well, by enforcing child support orders from the time they are determined by a court. But the program results vary greatly from state to state; this disparity weakens the program and needs careful scrutiny.

The National Forum Foundation recently conducted a study on the Child Support Enforcement program entitled, *Child Support*

*This essay draws from testimony given by the author before the United States Senate Finance Subcommittee on Social Security and Family Policy, in its hearing, "Welfare: Reform or Replacement?", February 20, 1987.

Enforcement: Unequal Protection Under the Law. The purpose of this report was to focus attention on the crisis faced by the nation's 8.4 million female-headed households, of which 5.5 million received no child support from the absent father in 1984, forcing millions of women and children into poverty. These single mothers and their children represent the fastest growing poverty group in America, a phenomenon commonly called "the feminization of poverty."

Our research and report, which has since been largely substantiated by the Office of Child Support Enforcement's (OCSE) 1985 Report to Congress, demonstrates that there is an enormous disparity among individual states' levels of performance in carrying out their responsibilities in the child support program. There are significant differences from one state to another in their success rates in establishing paternity, obtaining court orders for support, and collecting child support from the absent fathers.

For example, Table 1, illustrates the disparity of the states' performance in establishing paternity among the illegitimate children born in 1982. Michigan, Connecticut, Maryland, New Jersey, and Wisconsin led the nation by establishing paternity for about half of their paternity cases.

TABLE 1
4D PATERNITY ACTIONS FOR ILLEGITIMATE BIRTHS: 1982
(Sequenced by percent of illegitimate births normalized by paternity)

Rank	Illegitimate Births*	4D Paternity Actions**	% of Illegitimate Births
1 Michigan	22,378	12,952	57.9%
2 Connecticut	7,891	4,397	55.7%
3 Maryland	17,246	8,417	48.8%
4 New Jersey	21,425	9,647	45.0%
5 Wisconsin	11,188	5,025	44.9%
6 Utah	2,905	1,229	42.3%

TABLE 1 (Continued)

Rank	Illegitimate Births*	4D Paternity Actions**	% of Illegitimate Births
7 Tennessee	14,001	5,913	42.2%
8 No. Carolina	17,404	7,071	40.6%
9 Delaware	2,204	871	39.5%
10 Oregon	6,504	2,190	33.7%
11 Minnesota	8,427	2,707	32.1%
12 Alabama	13,996	4,472	32.0%
13 Hawaii	3,466	1,077	31.1%
14 Nevada	2,047	626	30.6%
15 Pennsylvania	31,224	9,362	30.0%
16 Ohio	31,070	8,552	27.5%
17 Kentucky	8,983	2,453	27.3%
18 Massachusetts	12,564	3,429	27.3%
19 Indiana	14,290	3,853	27.0%
20 Florida	35,422	8,870	25.0%
21 Maine	2,459	595	24.2%
U.S. AVERAGE			
22 Georgia	23,263	5,452	23.4%
24 Iowa	5,074	1,121	22.1%
25 North Dakota	1,318	284	21.5%
26 New York	63,298	12,751	20.1%
27 Vermont	1,184	234	19.8%
28 Dist. of Col.	5,004	941	18.8%
29 Kansas	5,278	978	18.5%
30 New Mexico	6,119	1,071	17.5%
31 Rhode Island	2,009	333	16.6%
32 Louisiana	20,210	3,273	16.2%
33 Virginia	15,981	2,463	15.4%
34 Arkansas	7,363	1,131	15.4%
35 Colorado	7,769	1,154	14.9%
36 Washington	9,997	1,474	14.7%
37 Illinois	42,695	6,194	14.5%
38 Oklahoma	8,204	1,132	13.8%

continued on next page

TABLE 1 (Continued)

Rank	Illegitimate Births*	4D Paternity Actions**	% of Illegit- imate Births
39 West Virginia	3,901	521	13.4%
40 Mississippi	13,605	1,751	12.9%
41 So. Carolina	12,595	1,413	11.2%
42 Wyoming	1,015	108	10.6%
43 Nebraska	3,434	335	9.8%
44 South Dakota	1,924	159	8.3%
45 Arizona	10,626	618	5.8%
46 Alaska	1,888	98	5.2%
47 Texas	41,447	1,862	4.5%
48 New Hampshire	1,734	64	3.7%
49 Missouri	14,395	424	2.9%
50 Montana	2,070	56	2.7%
51 Idaho	1,726	34	2.0%
U.S. TOTAL	715,227	172,564	24.1%

Source: *"Monthly Vital Statistics Report," 1982: Nat. Center for Health Statistics: Table 16.
**"Annual Report to Congress: 1982," (4D) p. 80.

On the other hand, nine states were unable to establish paternity for 90% or more of their paternity cases. The five states with the poorest performance (in 1982) were Idaho (2.0%), Montana (2.7%), Missouri (2.9%), New Hampshire (3.7%) and Texas (4.5%).

We find similar disparity when using several available standards to measure the efficiency of state child support programs. Table 2 lists the total CSE collections for each state in 1985. I have divided this dollar amount by the total number of CSE staff employed by that state on the last day of the fiscal year. We are left with a number representing the amount of child support collected by each state on a per-employee basis.

TABLE 2

	Total CSE Collections[1] 1985	Total Staff[2]	Collections Per Employee	Rank
Alabama	$ 25,532,365	341	$ 74,874	30
Alaska	10,794,100	94	114,511	15
Arizona	12,874,138	122	105,525	17
Arkansas	9,988,354	201	49,693	46
California	305,096,005	3,383	90,185	23
Colorado	18,324,030	323	56,730	44
Connecticut	48,209,627	149	323,554	3
Delaware	10,697,542	74	144,561	9
District of Columbia	4,692,401	147	31,921	54
Florida	45,751,133	705	64,895	39
Georgia	26,280,701	388	67,733	35
Guam	432,644	13	33,280	53
Hawaii	11,642,020	140	83,157	26
Idaho	5,814,561	72	80,757	28
Illinois	54,529,936	816	66,825	38
Indiana	33,683,169	388	86,812	24
Iowa	34,349,870	212	162,027	8
Kansas	11,429,798	239	47,823	49
Kentucky	25,144,526	374	67,281	36
Louisiana	34,258,854	768	44,607	51
Maine	14,120,830	119	118,662	13
Maryland	83,806,774	866	96,774	20
Massachusetts	98,339,241	343	286,703	4
Michigan	341,178,339	905	376,992	2
Minnesota	58,849,660	509	115,618	14
Mississippi	6,895,334	119	57,943	43
Missouri	36,716,460	341	107,672	16
Montana	3,906,279	48	81,380	27
Nebraska	29,905,975	166	180,156	6
Nevada	7,279,683	120	60,664	42
New Hampshire	12,771,173	72	177,877	7
New Jersey	200,155,498	1,454	137,658	11

continued on next page

TABLE 2 (Continued)

	Total CSE Collections[1] 1985	Total Staff[2]	Collections Per Employee	Rank
New Mexico	6,291,963	85	74,023	33
New York	199,550,391	2,326	85,791	25
North Carolina	45,042,203	659	68,349	34
North Dakota	3,645,370	51	71,477	32
Ohio	82,700,294	1,108	74,689	31
Oklahoma	9,233,358	196	47,108	50
Oregon	39,778,092	326	122,018	12
Pennsylvania	371,162,798	921	402,999	1
Puerto Rico	54,265,042	252	215,337	5
Rhode Island	8,633,782	82	105,290	18
South Carolina	11,062,658	118	93,751	21
South Dakota	3,153,548	47	67,096	37
Tennessee	23,562,038	365	64,553	40
Texas	30,311,364	474	63,948	41
Utah	16,758,601	296	56,616	45
Vermont	3,683,426	40	92,085	22
Virgin Islands	2,338,988	29	80,654	29
Virginia	16,277,731	334	48,735	48
Washington	56,829,556	560	101,481	19
West Virginia	4,690,694	112	41,881	52
Wisconsin	82,070,713	593	138,399	10
Wyoming	1,230,505	25	49,220	47
Totals	$2,695,724,138	23,010	$117,154	

1. Source: Form OCSE-34 Line 13 (A + B + C)
2. Source: Form OCSE-3 Lines G1 + G2 (AFDC + Non-AFDC)
   Staff levels as of September 30, 1985

I recognize that it would be premature to draw any conclusions from this number alone. But it is clearly an important performance indicator in assessing the relative and absolute performance of individual states' CSE bureaucracies.

To be specific, for every employee in Pennsylvania's statewide child support system $403,000 was collected in child support in FY 85. That same year, on the opposite side of the spectrum, for every employee in Washington D.C.'s program a mere $32,000 was collected in child support. Joining Pennsylvania at the top of the list are: Michigan, Connecticut and Massachusetts, all of which collected over $200,000 per employee. At the bottom of the scale along with the nation's capital are: Kansas, Virginia, Wyoming, and Arkansas - none of which collected over $50,000 per employee. Clearly there is a disparity between the productivity of the various systems. Why is this so?

A more common, and perhaps more telling, number used to measure the administrative efficiency of a state program is "total collections per dollar of administrative expenditures." This measure, along with other interesting data, is published in OCSE's 1985 Report to Congress, Volumes I and II. Counted among those states with particularly high ratings were: Michigan ($7.62 returned for each administrative dollar spent), Pennsylvania ($6.68), Nebraska ($6.32), Iowa ($5.92), and Delaware ($5.62). Among those with the lowest return on the government's investment are: the District of Columbia (with only $1.06 returned for every administrative dollar spent), Oklahoma and Guam ($1.46), Wyoming ($1.64), West Virginia ($1.66), and South Carolina ($1.70).

There is a further illustration of the disparity among the states' levels of performance. If we accept that an important goal of the CSE program is to transfer the burden of child support from the taxpayers to the absent father, Table 3 is instructive. This table identifies the total number of families removed from AFDC due to the effort of the state child support offices.

As you can see from the table, New York, New Jersey, Texas, and Tennessee were each able to free 2,000 to 6,000 families from AFDC dependency in 1985. During the same year Arizona, Guam, Maryland, Missouri, Vermont, Wyoming, and, once again, the District of Columbia were unsuccessful in removing a single family from AFDC.

Table 3
NUMBER OF FAMILIES REMOVED FROM AFDC
DUE TO CHILD SUPPORT COLLECTIONS

Alabama	324
Alaska	13
Arizona	0
Arkansas	109
California	445
Colorado	618
Connecticut	667
Delaware	54
District of Columbia	0
Florida	305
Georgia	1,600
Guam	0
Hawaii	140
Idaho	38
Illinois	615
Indiana	154
Iowa	21
Kansas	194
Kentucky	257
Louisiana	645
Maine	197
Maryland	0
Massachusetts	1,258
Michigan	570
Minnesota	808
Mississippi	68
Missouri	0
Montana	53
Nebraska	23
Nevada	79
New Hampshire	28
New Jersey	4,386
New Mexico	51
New York	6,105
North Carolina	145

TABLE 3 (Continued)

North Dakota	1,673
Ohio	226
Oklahoma	101
Oregon	113
Pennsylvania	665
Puerto Rico	1,032
Rhode Island	282
South Carolina	1,867
South Dakota	36
Tennessee	2,730
Texas	2,851
Utah	647
Vermont	0
Virgin Islands	1
Virginia	111
Washington	0
West Virginia	689
Wisconsin	903
Wyoming	0
Nationwide Totals	33,897

Source: Form OCSE-3 Line E1 (AFDC)

Here again, it would be wrong to rely on one chart. There is much we do not know about CSE program performance. In that connection it is unfortunate that there is much we *cannot* know, given the limits of the annual OCSE statistical reports to Congress. In many key performance categories it provides absolute numbers in illustrating states' performance, but no data that would allow us to make useful state-by-state comparisons. We know, for example, that Florida and Missouri each established paternity for some 14,400 in 1985. But how many paternity cases did these states contend with that year? In the absence of this data it is impossible to measure the relative performance of the states in this and other vital CSE categories. The publication of such important data would greatly assist the effort to evaluate and improve the CSE program.

While this is only a minute sampling of the data available, it suggests that some states are performing very well, others marginally, and others poorly in collecting child support.

In truth, we should be encouraged by these findings because those state, county, and local offices across America that are doing a good job have shattered any illusions that the child support program is too complex, too burdensome, or too underfunded to operate efficiently. Our task now is to carefully examine this nation's child support machine and all of its parts to determine why the machine works so much better in Detroit, Fresno, and Indianapolis than in other cities.

To my knowledge no government agency or independent institution has conducted a comprehensive and comparative analysis to assess the reasons why states' performance is so varied. This analysis must be done. Common sense tells us that if we can identify those characteristics which distinguish the efficient CSE offices from the others, the lessons learned will pay dividends if applied to all state programs.

The vast differences we have observed among the states cannot easily be explained away as the result of demographic or economic circumstances unique to a particular region. On the contrary our survey suggests that there is no clear correlation between a state being urban or rural or the condition of its economy, and the performance of its CSE program. We must suspect that there are real differences among the state and local programs in terms of how effectively they are administered and how vigorously they pursue their goals. We cannot overlook the possibility that the problem is one of local management. At the same time, I am persuaded that we need additional information before proposing any new programs or major modifications. Therefore, with the intention of improving the CSE program, we recommend that Congress, the GAO, and the Office of Child Support Enforcement work together to accomplish the following:

1. Conduct a comprehensive comparative analysis of state CSE programs to determine the key performance factors or indicators that could measure the relative performance of the

states. This study should seek to ascertain CSE performance data at not only the state but the local level, inasmuch as: a) no public data describing the performance at the county or local level exists; and b) it is highly probable that certain county programs with heavy caseloads have a disproportionate and distortive impact on their state's overall performance.

2. Apply the lessons learned from this analysis to provide guidelines and standardized procedures for state and local program administrators.

3. Determine CSE "industry averages" and establish minimum performance standards in all areas of accountability.

4. Develop an incentive program that rewards top performers (both the states and outstanding individual employees) and that penalizes those states failing to meet the standards. The current "incentive" system automatically rewards each of the fifty state CSE programs, along with those of the District of Columbia, Guam, and Puerto Rico. Nearly $600,000,000 was paid in the incentive program from 1981 through 1985; no state or jurisdiction failed to receive an incentive payment in any of those five years. The extent to which such a system encourages the improvement of the least effective programs is highly questionable.

Table 4
INCENTIVE PAYMENTS

Alabama	3,023,616
Alaska	277,661
Arizona	190,908
Arkansas	748,666
California	20,276,143
Colorado	1,121,093
Connecticut	2,906,140
Delaware	461,687
District of Columbia	297,029

continued on next page

TABLE 4 (Continued)

Florida	3,453,057
Georgia	2,311,947
Guam	28,637
Hawaii	700,365
Idaho	499,222
Illinois	2,767,448
Indiana	2,975,974
Iowa	2,803,578
Kansas	1,099,984
Kentucky	1,071,940
Louisiana	1,461,320
Maine	1,253,225
Maryland	3,088,697
Massachusetts	5,572,707
Michigan	14,581,657
Minnesota	3,677,410
Mississippi	366,218
Missouri	2,146,283
Montana	363,090
Nebraska	690,742
Nevada	154,498
New Hampshire	290,944
New Jersey	5,886,770
New Mexico	449,894
New York	9,497,632
North Carolina	2,808,500
North Dakota	314,821
Ohio	5,710,194
Oklahoma	786,774
Oregon	1,624,279
Pennsylvania	6,788,209
Puerto Rico	167,382
Rhode Island	613,134
South Carolina	1,015,453
South Dakota	226,508
Tennessee	715,706
Texas	1,877,920

TABLE 4 (Continued)

Utah	729,867
Vermont	379,061
Virgin Islands	25,311
Virginia	1,658,179
Washington	3,672,621
West Virginia	537,889
Wisconsin	4,986,454
Wyoming	90,319
Nationwide Totals	131,224,763

Source: Form OCSE-34 Line 16 (A + B)

Child Support Enforcement is not a partisan issue. Those states that rank high and low indicate that this problem transcends all political, racial, economic and social lines.

The principal beneficiaries of increased enforcement measures will be the women and children on whose behalf the state will act. It was for the sake of children that the AFDC program was established, and child support enforcement ensures that parental responsibility remains a social value in attaining this goal. The well-being of children today, based upon this primary reliance of parents can tend toward the hope of preventing a new cycle of poverty in the future.

COURTING DISASTER: WELFARE AND THE FEDERAL JUDICIARY

William J. Gribbin

In recent years, we seem to have made a breakthrough in public policy concerning poverty and public assistance programs simply by the creeping realization that poverty means more than lack of cash. In retrospect, so much of the Great Society was based on that curious notion: they fancy that, if only the poor had what others have—or as much as others have—then they wouldn't be poor anymore. That was a cardinal tenet of the liberal *ancien regime,* just as it is a liberal tenet of certain cardinals even today.

Consider, for example, the mischief of a concept like "the poverty line." We've always known that it is a theoretical construct, an approximation, a fiction in fact, though a necessary one for all sorts of programmatic and administrative purposes. And it is necessary, too, because the policy process in a modern state cannot cope with anything that is not quantified. That, by the way, may have been the secret of David Stockman's power when he was steering welfare policy in official Washington: he could quantify anything, replacing complicated values with more complicated numbers. But this is one phenomenon we should not blame on Mr. Stockman. After all, for at least a quarter of a century, Congress' fascination with poverty lines and other measurements of income has reflected an underlying assumption—a doctrine, really—from which few have dared to dissent. To wit, poverty has been a function of economics.

Yes, poverty does have something to do with income. But at long last, many are starting to realize that it can have as much, or more, to do with other matters. Like culture. The very term "underclass," after all, is not so much an economic category as a social description. This new awareness is a vital step toward the definition and eventual correction of what went wrong with the domestic programs of the Great Society.

We are not, of course, speaking of the poverty that exists among the abandoned elderly, among injured breadwinners, or among persons trapped in low-income jobs that do not adequately sustain their households. Today's discussion focuses upon the poverty culture, the long-term poor, especially the multi-generational poor: the people described in Charles Murray's article in *National Review*.[1]

Nicholas Lemann's study in *The Atlantic Monthly*[2] of Chicago poverty and its Mississippi roots hit the same theme, explicitly making a point which should be carved someday into the tombstones of the Great Society's tacticians: that any one-dimensional analysis of poverty as an economic phenomenon misses the heart of the matter.

It would be naive to think that official Washington, confronted with naysayers like Murray and Lemann, will wise up and admit it has wasted billions of dollars and two generations of human potential by its obsession with economic factors. The welfare industry cannot possibly face poverty as a symptom of a defective culture (in the anthropological sense of a pattern of values, behavioral norms, standards, shared beliefs, attitudes and expectations). No official religion ever disestablishes itself.

Most of the Congress remains mired in the not terribly significant debate over who can best create jobs—liberal advocates of public training programs or less liberal advocates of enterprise zones, regulatory reform, and investment incentives, as if jobs, once created, can themselves generate a more stable lifestyle, a goal-oriented attitude, an end to the dysfunctional personal behavior that characterizes the poverty culture wherever it appears, north or south, in neighborhoods black or white, or on Indian reservations.

This is not a criticism of job creation. It is the engine of all sorts of progress, both economic and more important kinds. But it works at the end of an acculturation process, a process about which virtually no one in official Washington wants to talk, perhaps because it shows how superficial and trivial have been most of our efforts to transform the lives of the long-term poor. Perhaps, too, because it compels us to assert absolutes—the ultimate *faux pas* in a society which tolerates almost any outrage except unequivocal belief. It requires us to be culturally intolerant, judgmental, preferential, doctrinaire. It means we have to say we *know* how people should live, and in what familial arrangements, if they are to be productive, self-fulfilled citizens. We now, and for their own sakes, we will see to it that they do live that way. As I noted, that's an unpopular view, but one which may be gaining ground in policy closets all over town—simply because all else has failed.

It had to fail eventually, for it was built on faulty intellectual assumptions about some fairly important things, including human nature. It was only partially accidental that the Great Society's social engineering came at the same time as the youth follies of the 1960s and the sexual revolution. No, Lyndon Johnson did not breed the counterculture or provoke widespread promiscuity. But those social distortions were nonetheless related to his era of governmental expansion and experiment. All resulted from a broader shift of culture, a deeper turn of mind. The social policies of the 1960s and 1970s—yes, the '70s too, for we must not forget who was the presidential proponent of the Family Assistance Program—were symptoms, just as ruined housing projects, drug abuse, porn and teen pregnancy have been symptoms of the same underlying malady.

That malady has been cultural relativism, the triumph of positivism in public affairs: the sophistication manque of policy amorality, environmentalism, a developmental view of human nature. That view is far more important than amounts of money among the poor, whether they be incentives or disincentives. For it cuts off individuals and the body politic which they together constitute from certitudes, absolutes, assurance and the ability to act upon it in public matters.

We think of the Great Society in two stereotypes. One is President Johnson standing before the Congress, calling for this and that. The other is Congress itself, eagerly accepting his invitation to expand its purview and expend the public's resources. Who's missing? Who has been missing all these years in our analysis of the aftermath of the Great Society? The Judiciary, for the Federal courts have done at least as much to advance the agenda of the Great Society as did its inventors in the Executive and its abettors in the Legislature. And most important, the Great Society jurists are the only part of that regime still with us, active and ambitious as ever.

First, a definition: "Great Society judge" is not a partisan term. It applies to many jurists whose tenure began before that of President Johnson and many others named long after his departure from office. It includes Republicans. It is as much a cultural term as a political one. It is shorthand for those judges who operate in the legal sphere from the same premise which underlay the Great Society programs: that social progress is a function, not of personal improvement through adherence to unchanging moral norms, but of enlightened tinkering by a credentialed class of power-wielding improvers. That, I think, is a fair exposition of the official mind-set that shaped the Great Society in the early 1960s and perpetuated its legacy thereafter. It is, needless to say, pure Comte, though not one in a thousand of its practitioners would know what that means.

It would be fascinating, though outside the scope of these modest remarks, to see what number of President Carter's judicial nominees developed their political standing within the Great Society framework as its bureaucrats, rule writers, legislators, grantees, counsellors, state cheerleaders, and program attorneys. Ironically, through their disproportionate presence on the Federal bench—since Mr. Carter appointed such a large proportion of sitting jurists—these younger judges have perpetuated the Great Society long after it was deemed moribund. It reminds one of those bizarre sci-fi flicks in which a frozen monster returns from the dead: Great Society II, back and meaner than ever.

Indeed, as far as our legal system is concerned, the Great Society never lapsed. It yet controls much of public policy: crime, family relations, roles of men and women, child rearing, a broad range of ethical issues concerning reproductive behavior, religious expression, and basically what a community can expect or demand from individuals within it. What does all that have to do with poverty? Everything, for those items are the warp and woof of culture. For millennia, observers of the human condition have focused on those factors—family life, character formation, the power of the polis to define virtue and to enforce at least its appearance—as the determinants of public order and individual happiness.

Those factors are today the areas of public policy still managed—the word is appropriately vague—by Great Society judges. No wonder that the last quarter century of court intervention in those areas has been the explicit judicial analog to the axioms implicit in the legislative and executive programs of the Great Society. It has been the denial of norms, the striking down of verities, indeed of the very concept of verity. It has been sheer relativism, the annihilation of culture by an anti-culture that, like a black hole, swallows up all strictures, all absolutes, except, of course, absolutely "equal protection of the law," whatever that means from day to day.

The judicial Great Society has meant the disappearance of normative standards, the kind of communal ordering of daily life which, once upon a time, could limit the number of people who were headed toward dependency; the standards, in other words, the absence of which makes the underclass the underclass— everything from the expectation of regular labor to not littering, from avoidance of substance abuse to close supervision of one's offspring, from a personal association with the common good to reproductive responsibility, from the expectation that punishment follows crime to the assumption that rewards follow merit.

Nothing the Great Society planners devised legislatively has had a more deleterious effect than what the Great Society jurists have done in this regard. For examples, we can turn to the roster of decisions in which the Supreme Court has pulled the props out from under the social order by forbidding states, localities, or the Congress to define or enforce that order. *Griswold* v. *Connecticut, Boddie* v. *Connecticut, Zablocki* v. *Redhail, Eisenstadt* v. *Baird* had the cumulative effect of abolishing the traditional authority of the state to regulate marriage and sexual activity. Against that backdrop, *Roe* v. *Wade* and its sequellae should have surprised no one.

King v. *Smith, New Jersey Welfare Rights Organization* v. *Cahill*, and *USDA* v. *Moreno* gutted attempts to enforce the moral order of the family as the basis for public assistance. *Levy* v. *Louisiana, Glona* v. *American Guarantee and Liability Insurance Company, Gomez* v. *Perez*, and *Weber* v. *Aetna Casualty and Surety Company* put an end to legal distinctions between legitimacy and illegitimacy or, more accurately, to legal preference for the former. *Moore* v. *City of East Cleveland* denied to the citizens of that predominantly black community the power to zone their town for intact families, thereby protecting residents from the downward drag of the welfare culture. In so doing, *Moore* in effect forbade any community in America to define "family" in a traditional way.[3]

The positivism of the Great Society has triumphed. The family is outside the law. That is, family relationships may not be given preferential standing in law. Marriage can have no special status. Divorce no opprobrium or impediment. Illegitimacy no problems. We are all autonomous individuals, whatever our living arrangements, cut off—we might say, liberated—from howsoever many millennia of human experience about what works for human happiness and what causes misery. Ironic, isn't it, that while welfare policy analysts were debating the effects of the 33-and-a-third income exclusion for determining AFDC eligibility and benefits, the Great Society courts virtually wiped out the legal basis of the family. Which issue, I wonder, was more important over the long run in increasing the size of the underclass and crippling movement out of dependency? We have carefully charted the risky streams but neglected the tidal wave bearing down upon us.

It is currently fashionable, across the ideological spectrum, to consider strong family life as the best antidote to poverty and to admit that weak family situations have something to do with the poverty trap. But that modest agreement is only the first step toward reform, and the second step is not a popular one. It is just this: to face the fact that the Great Society courts have left public policy almost powerless to fortify family life, enforce familial obligations, demand family responsibility, protect family rights, or enhance family identity.

Once we face up to that situation, then we must ask what is the real anti-poverty agenda of the 1980s and beyond. Clearly, it is not to strike poses of concern for the family, not to engage in the rhetorical blather that takes the place of substantive action. That agenda may include job creation, self-help efforts, work requirements, eliminating disincentives to advancement, and ensuring adequate benefits to the needy. But all of those together will not be sufficient to reverse the growth of the poverty culture and to tilt the balance of public policy back in favor of the family. No, for those purposes, we must lift the dead hand of the Great Society from the courts.

Breaking that hold means returning to communities and to the national community the authority to set norms and affirm values. It means cleansing the courts of what Robert Bork has called "ideologies that are subversive of the very idea of the rule of law."[4] It means enforcing, by whatever means are appropriate and available, judicical respect for the bourgeois family order undermined by Great Society programs and still contemned by Great Society courts.

What I am sugesting is that it does little good to trash Great Society legislation unless we repudiate as well its philosophical premises, particularly the positivist notion that there is no natural order of society and no inherently right patterns of living, loving, begetting and getting through life. It is easy to disavow CETA, for example, and to denounce the many excesses of "the poverty program," however it be defined. It takes more courage to reject the intellectual assumptions that shaped those programs and their era.

That involves repudiating a whole train of jurisprudence that has negated the interest of the state in defining and enforcing the marriage contract. It involves affirming the right of the people, through their legislators, to protect themselves and the body politic against moral harm, as well as economic. It means holding accountable, not only the footloose males or the underclass, but their more affluent counterparts whose search for greener, or younger, pastures has done so much to generate the New Poor, the women and children left needy by the breakup of the home.

It means, in fact, being intolerant, not unsympathetic but intolerant of personal deviations, intolerant of dysfunctional culture, intolerant of behavior that erodes family life and thereby erodes the fast track out of dependency.

It is important for us today to review the legacy of the Great Society in its legislative and executive aspects. But it is more important to realize that what *was* done by those branches of government was small potatoes compared to what still is being done by the judiciary, which imposes upon us all, poor and non-poor alike, a poverty of spirit, a deprivation of values, a desperate neediness in home and family life, a void of faith where there should be the strongest certitude.

I do not know to what extent escape from poverty may be facilitated by purely economic measures, of Right or of Left. But it would be folly to think we can get away with that limited approach, without also undertaking the reestablishment of the bourgeois family order and the recreation of a judicial system that respects and, to a degree, enforces it.

NOTES

[1]Charles Murray, "White Welfare, White Families, 'White Trash'," *National Review,* (March 28, 1986), pp. 30-34.
[2]Nicholas Lemann, "The Origins of the Underclass," *Atlantic* (June, 1986), pp. 31-55.
[3]Carl A. Anderson, "The Family in Contemporary Constitutional Law," paper delivered to Symposium on the Family, Marquette University (February 19, 1985). I am especially indebted to Professor Anderson's studies of the Court's decisions concerning the status of the family and the marital bond.
[4]Robert H. Bork, "Tradition and Morality in Constitutional Law," The Francis Boyer Lecture of 1984 (Washington, D.C.: American Enterprise Institute, 1984), p. 2.

WELFARE SPENDING AND THE POVERTY RATE

Richard Vedder

On August 20, 1964, President Lyndon Johnson, at the signing ceremony for the first anti-poverty bill, announced that the ". . . days of the dole in this country are numbered."

When the President left office five years later, the feeling was widespread that Johnson perhaps was right. The proportion of Americans officially described as poor had fallen thirty-six percent by 1969, and at the same time an almost precise doubling of per capita federal real public aid expenditure for lower income groups in that five years was felt to have had a very substantial payoff.

Fifteen years passed. The Great Society programs continued to expand so that real public aid extended by the federal government more than doubled again, yet the poverty rate, officially measured, stopped falling and, indeed, was almost twenty percent higher in 1984 than in 1969.

Even allowing for the distortions in poverty rate that were introduced from using a faulty price index, the poverty rate by the early '80s had shown no real improvement over the late '60s, despite annual expenditure increases of tens of billions of dollars.

In a detailed statistical investigation of the public assistance poverty relationship performed with Lowell Gallaway, we have concluded that since about 1972, increased expenditures of public assistance have actually served to increase, not decrease, the rate of poverty in the United States, as the income-increasing effects of larger entitlements are more than offset by the income-retarding effects of work disincentives introduced by the relatively generous welfare system.

Using an analytic device which we call the Poverty-Welfare curve, we note a C-shaped curve where federal public aid expenditures for the disadvantaged beyond about 40 or 45 billion dollars, on balance actually increased poverty by inducing people to avoid employment income. We called this "poverty by choice," and one estimate is that about 5,700,000 poor Americans in 1984 fell into this category.

To conclude that increased welfare spending has actually increased the poverty rate is startling and it is certainly not a very fashionable statement, particularly in Washington. I believe it is true that we have a rather unique and dubious distinction of having been the only persons in recent years that had our findings consciously suppressed from publication by both the *Washington Post* and the Cato Institute. The left finds these results objectionable because they imply federal public assistance spending is ineffective and should be reduced. Some persons on the right, on the other hand, find the results objectionable may because acceptance of them may incur the enmity of so-called respectable members of the academic establishment, or possibly because economic growth has not eliminated the problem, as conservatives had generally asserted it would.

In any case, the causal relationship between public assistance spending and measured poverty observed when assistance levels are relatively high holds no matter how you measure it. If you measure welfare spending on a per capita basis, or per recipient basis, or if one incorporates state and local expenditures into the assistance measure, you get the same relationship. In fact, the perverse public assistance effects are observed when, instead of looking at poverty rate, one looks at the income distribution as a whole; that is, the Gini coefficient.

Similarly, the relationship holds if one uses John Weicher's estimates adjusting for inappropriate measures of inflation; or if one uses a poverty rate estimate that incorporates the cash value of non-cash governmental payment.

Similarly, it holds for different age and sex cohorts, although far more so for ones for whom labor force participation is a real option.

In one exercise, we ran some 384 different variants of the poverty-welfare relationship, and in every single case, the observed relationship was obtained, in most cases indicating that somewhere between 1970 and 1973 the threshold was passed whereby additional public assistance induced more poverty than it eliminated.

Principles for Change

Professor Gallaway and I considered possible changes in the system, and certainly any reform is not going to be easy. I do not know that we have any answers, and it remains easier to point out the problems than come up with solutions.

Six principles might be considered in any welfare reform, for possible future discussion.

First and most important, the implicit marginal tax rate on work must be sharply reduced for the poor. For many recipients of welfare, the welfare payment loss from working equals 50 or 75 or even 100 percent of their income. High marginal tax rates destroy work incentives, and we now in this country implicitly tax the work income of the poor far more than the rich. The conservative way to change this is to reduce maximum benefit levels, but also reduce the amount of public assistance payments lost for any incremental work-related income. The liberal way to solve this problem would be to keep maximum benefit levels the same but stretch out welfare eligibility into higher income brackets.

Second, we believe that relatively generous support should be maintained for those who cannot work, for whom work is not an alternative owing to disability. We are a compassionate people, and we can afford to help those who are unable to help themselves. At the same time, however, it is not unreasonable to define and verify disability in a relatively hardnosed fashion to eliminate abuse.

A third possible principle that welfare reform should incorporate relates to the fact the majority of the welfare payments in the AFDC program go to long-term beneficiaries. To reduce long-term welfare dependency and also free up funds to more generously help those who are temporarily in need, perhaps some consideration should be given to actually gradually reducing benefits the longer an individual receives them. In other words, the implicit marginal tax rate for working should decline over time in order to encourage labor force participation. Perhaps the unemployment compensation model should be followed; where benefits are cut off after six months or so. Under this approach, welfare payments could be viewed as a short-term safety net, not a lifetime income source.

Fourth, more control over public charity should be given the state and local governments, which also should be given more flexibility to experiment with alternative assistance delivery systems in order to enhance our knowledge of the impact of different policies. We've got a great opportunity to experiment here. Perhaps some experimentation should be encouraged with giving local welfare officials a free hand in evaluating eligibility, giving performance bonuses for those officials who demonstrate that they have reduced measured poverty in relatively large amounts per dollar. There are many problems with such a program, but a large part of those who are poor receive little or no assistance, while many of the non-poor absorb a goodly portion of scarce welfare funds. Attempting to encourage welfare entrepreneurship of a socially useful nature would seem desirable.

A fifth principle we might consider is that public policy should encourage private philanthropy. There is some evidence that dollar-for-dollar, private assistance has a greater payoff in eliminating poverty than public funds. There is also some evidence that there is a crowding out of private philanthropy by public aid. Private charities can reduce overhead, avoid the rigid eligibility requirements and are often more knowledgeable about the true condition of individuals and can adjust aid accordingly with a minimum of red tape.

The sixth principle deals with the problem of teen-age illegitimacy, and suggests that perhaps we should just simply eliminate aid for minors. It has been proposed by the Reagan Administration. Moreover, perhaps in some states, it is worth noting that the marginal revenue (using economics jargon), for unwed mothers associated with having children actually exceeds the marginal cost for raising those children. Up to a point, having children is literally profitable financially. That should be ended. We are possibly the only major nation in the world that explicitly rewards teenage promiscuity. The whole concept of relating aid to the production of illegitimate children should be re-examined.

Now, the principles we espouse are inherently compatible with either conservative or liberal principles. Alternative approaches to implementation are available, some that cost far less than current policy, but others that actually increase our resources that go to this area. Given our past dismal record, we tend to favor the less expensive, more conservative approaches. But above all, we favor reducing the massive disincentives to working and forming traditional family arrangements implicit in the current welfare system.

Perhaps we should return to the principles advocated in the mid-60s when the war on poverty began; namely, we should use public aid to lend a helping hand, a hand that helps the poor take care off themselves.

HOUSING: THE FIRST AND LAST GREAT SOCIETY PROGRAM

John C. Weicher

Housing policy is not often thought of as part of the Great Society, but the first "Great Society" program was a housing program: public housing, enacted almost 30 years before the term was coined. And the last Great Society programs were housing ones, Sections 235 and 236, enacted so late in the Johnson Administration that for all practical purposes they began under his successor—and ended under him, as well.

Indeed, the history of housing policy offers a new angle for considering the Great Society. There were lessons to be learned when the Great Society was created—lessons that were largely ingored—and implications for the evaluation of its achievements and failures.

Public Housing

Public housing was originally advocated as a way of helping the poor to resolve their social problems, to become part of mainstream of society. As far back as the turn of the century, reformers were pointing out that slums were breeding grounds for all the ills of urban society: crime, delinquency, disease, death, mental illness, and more. The reformers felt that if you got rid of the slums, you'd get rid of the problems. When the National Housing Act was passed in 1937, there was an endless parade of

77

witnesses who thought public housing was the way to solve these problems. The conventional wisdom of the day comes out clearly in a Senate Committee Report in 1937, accompanying the bill:

> "At a cost much cheaper than the terrible social and business toll of unhealthful housing—in terms of disease, crime, and maladjustment—it will provide better living quarters for millions who now dwell in dismal and insanitary conditions.
>
> The acute shortage of decent, safe and sanitary dwellings within the financial reach of families of low income is:
>
> Inimical to the general welfare of the Nation by:
>
> (a) encouraging the spread of disease and lowering the level of health, morale, and vitality of large portions of the American people;
>
> (b) increasing the hazards of fire, accidents, and natural calamities;
>
> (c) subjecting the moral standards of the young to bad influences;
>
> (d) impairing industrial and agricultural productive efficiency;
>
> (e) increasing the violation of the criminal laws of the United States and of the several states;
>
> (f) lowering the standards of living of large portions of the American people;
>
> (g) necessitating a vast and extraordinary expenditure of public funds, Federal, State, and local, for crime prevention, punishment and correction, fire protection, public-health service, and relief."

All that was going to be taken care of by public housing, but it didn't take long to be disabused. There really was not much of a public housing program until after World War II, despite that stirring rhetoric; the program didn't get started on a substantial scale until the beginning of the war, and then it became a vehicle for war worker housing. But after the war came the big apartment projects that we now think of as public housing, as well as a lot of low-rise and row-house projects.

We quickly found out that all these good things weren't happening. "We" isn't just the conservative Southern Democrats and Old Guard Republicans who had always opposed public housing, "we" includes—particularly includes—the people who had advocated public housing and who were running it. Within ten or fifteen years, many of these people knew it didn't work. Some of the bitterest criticisms came from the original true believers.

Public housing tenants had their criticisms as well:

> Nobody cared what we wanted when they built this place. They threw our houses down and pushed us here and pushed our friends somewhere else. We don't have a place around here to get a cup of coffee or a newspaper even, or borrow fifty cents. Nobody cared what we need. But the big men come and look at that grass [the large lawn in front of the project] and say, 'Isn't it wonderful! Now the poor have everything!

Utopia didn't come to pass when the government put up a nice new twenty-story apartment building with a big expanse of grass around it.

By 1961, Jane Jacobs could refer matter-of-factly to "low-income projects that have become worse centers of delinquency, vandalism, and general social hopelessness than the slums they were supposed to replace." And while her book, *The Death and Life of Great American Cities,* was controversial, nobody argued with that part of it. (Her book also contains the quotation from the East Harlem tenant.) Several years later, President Johnson's National Commission on Urban Problems, chaired by former Senator Paul Douglas of Illinois, acknowledged unhappily the existence of "multi-problem families" in public housing, and suggested half-heartedly that project designs might be part of the problem—designs which had been the height of architectural fashion less than two decades before.

Nonetheless, the belief in housing died hard. During the Watts riots, some Eastern journalists were considerably startled when they found that Watts consisted of small single-family housing on separate lots, and wondered why poor people would riot when they lived so well. Perhaps the solution was to be found in better housing programs.

To find them, President Johnson appointed two commissions: one on urban housing, chaired by Edgar Kaiser, the other, previously mentioned, on urban problems generally, which took housing and related programs as its province also. Out of their deliberations eventually came the distinctive Great Society housing programs. Section 235 subsidized the mortgages for poor people to buy small homes, both new and existing houses, and Section 236 provided similar subsidies for developers to put up apartment projects. These programs were not really for the poor, but rather for people who were *almost* eligible for public housing. Their purpose was not so much to remove slums as to create good housing in the suburbs for the near-poor.

One feature of these programs is especially noteworthy. They provided an inducement for private lenders to issue the mortgages by offering FHA mortgage insurance. If the homeowner or the developer defaulted on the mortgage, the government paid off the mortgage and took over the property. These were big programs; from 1968 to 1973 they amounted to over half a million units. This was about half as many public housing units as had been built in the previous thirty-five years combined.

These projects were an improvement on public housing in that they didn't have social problems, although they didn't particularly seem to solve social problems either. However, they had financial problems, and scandals. In several places, individuals and firms bought up old rundown houses, gave them cosmetic repairs, bribed an appraiser or HUD functionary, and sold them through the Section 235 program to poor people. They moved in and the roof fell in—literally—and they couldn't afford to fix it.

Even without fraud, many low-income homeowners had trouble making the subsidized mortgage payments. Operating costs in apartment projects proved to be too high for many tenants to pay out of their own incomes. Management often proved to be difficult and unexpectedly expensive.

With FHA insurance, the financial problems of homeowners and project sponsors became the federal government's problems. As they defaulted, the government kept getting title to more and more houses and apartment projects, and Congress had to start appropriating money directly to pay off the mortgages.

By 1972 everybody knew that something had to be done. George Romney was HUD secretary and he urged President Nixon to stop the programs; in early 1973 the President did. He suspended public housing at the same time. And Congress—a Democratic Congress—tacitly agreed.

Thus, housing subsidy programs were both the first and the last Great Society programs to be created. They were the first to be stopped. They were acknowledged failures. The key word is "acknowledged." There are several yardsticks to measure housing programs against, and by these yardsticks most analysts and policymakers could see the program failure plainly.

One is FHA insurance. It is unique among federal subsidy programs. It was clear when programs didn't work because the failures came right back into the hands of the federal government. Moreover, the failure rate of Section 235 and 236 could be compared to failure rates for the basic FHA programs to promote home ownership and provide housing for middle-income Americans. For the near-poor, it was a lot higher. One of the best reasons for continuing FHA is this automatic monitor on housing subsidies; the failures come home to roost.

Second is the fact that housing assistance was not an entitlement. Because it was so expensive to build subsidized housing—either public housing or Sections 235 and 236—very few poor people were able to live in subsidized housing, even after thirty-five years of public housing. This was unfair to the large majority of the poor. In compensation—to policymakers if not to the poor themselves—it facilitated program evaluation. There was one set of poor people who weren't being helped by the government living in private housing; and a set who were, living in subsidized housing. The poor were gradually improving their housing, decade by decade, to a much greater extent than could possibly be attributed to subsidized housing programs. "Moderate income people" and even fairly poor people were finding decent housing in the private market—expensive, but decent. The Census Bureau surveyed the population every ten years and showed us that we were gradually meeting our housing quality standards. Substandard housing dropped from about 45 percent of all housing in 1940 to about 8 percent in 1970. It dropped for the poor, for blacks, for the elderly, for everybody.

One of the great differences between housing and other programs is the presence of these yardsticks. It is fairly easy to see what worked and what didn't. In others, such as Operation Head Start, yardsticks are absent. My colleagues who study pre-school programs for children believe the programs do not work well, but they really only have first-hand evidence from the specific projects they know about, and anecdotal evidence. There are very few well-regarded evaluations and they only cover a small sample of programs. So the programs go on.

There is one final and disturbing lesson from housing policy. Charles Murray does not consider housing in *Losing Ground,* because the data were not detailed enough for his purposes, but the housing changes seen are consistent with the data he reports, in my judgment. In reading his book, I saw a distinction between economic and social phenomena. The nation has been getting richer and doing better economically—the poor as well—and there isn't much of an economic break after 1965. That seems to be true about the incidence of poverty as well as overall well-being. But we are doing worse in so many social dimensions—crime and illegitimacy, for examples—and in dimensions that are both economic and social, like educational attainment. In the 1960s, we fell off a cliff in these social respects as documented by Murray. People have argued about his explanation, but not too many people about his data. The Great Society may not have caused the problem; as my colleague Ben Wattenberg is fond of saying, "There was no Soft on Crime Act of 1965." But it sure didn't prevent it.

Housing fits this pattern. In the 1930s, the informed opinion was that economic and social phenomena were really the same; if we could solve the economic problems, the social ones would take care of themselves. Now we know better. We are better housed than we dreamed of 40 and 50 years ago. But the social problems that better housing was supposed to solve—the litany of the Senate Report in 1937—are largely still there.

AN OPPORTUNITY APPROACH TO ALLEVIATING POVERTY

William Orzechowski

Disappointment with traditional approaches to poverty has led to considerable re-thinking. We have spent enormous sums of money, yet the results are not very impressive. Poverty rates are not too much different from what they were in the middle 1960's when the great surge in federal aid began. Over the long haul, progress has been made. Franklin D. Roosevelt commented that in his time almost one person in three was in a poverty situation. Today, when all cash and in-kind benefits are considered, this rate has dropped to about seven percent. Yet the poverty rate when a number of the in-kind benefits are excluded has stayed around the fifteen percent rate over the past twenty years and many problems such as crime, unemployment, and dependency persist.

As a consequence, many are turning to a different model of human behavior. In some ways we are discovering common sense. We are coming to realize that it is difficult to spend our way out of poverty; Robert Woodson said, "when fairness is defined in terms of how much we spend, the poor are the real losers." At present, there is greater emphasis placed upon individual incentives. Greater reliance is placed upon creating opportunity by unleashing the innate abilities and talents of individuals in poverty. The stress is on creating ambition and motivation for those in poverty to work hard, take risks, save and invest.

There is a great deal of merit in this approach. Thomas Sowell's analysis of ethnic groups suggests that those groups that have had the greatest economic success are those that exploit opportunities in the private sector. They are groups where a strong work ethic is part of the culture. He found that those groups that relied on the political process for material gain did not fare as well. His work in many respects parallels the famous study by Louis Worth who came up with similar conclusions in his analysis of the amazing success of the Jewish people in prevailing against formidable barriers. On a larger scale one can see the same process at work in comparing the record of nations around the world. For example, the case of Hong Kong versus Mexico. The former is a free enterprise economy, the latter is an over-regulated economy. While Hong Kong's economic progress is a marvel of the world, many are stumped at Mexico's stagnation in spite of its great base of natural resources.

The emphasis, then, on the private sector as the way to alleviate poverty is a very important one. In order to accomplish this it is important to both create business and job opportunities within the private sector and get those in poverty to exploit those opportunities by taking advantage and nurturing the innate abilities they possess. A blueprint for achieving this objective will no doubt change as we grope with the problem but there are a number of initiatives that can be undertaken to get more of the poor into the private sector and eventually out of poverty.

Creating Opportunities

At the outset it is important to stress the role that economic growth can play. Many often downplay the importance of economic growth by stating that it often by-passes those in poverty. Yet there is a great deal of merit in the principle that "all boats can rise together." The truth is that few social problems can be solved in a stagnating economy. James P. Smith and Finis Welch, in a study conducted for the U.S. Department of Labor, show that 45% of the reduction in black poverty since 1940 was due to economic growth. They comment that if economic growth could have continued at the same rate in the 1970's as it did during the 1960's, the black poverty rate would have fallen another 25%.

The secrets of economic growth have been well known since the days of the Founding Fathers. It requires moderate taxation, limited government, and a minimum of burdensome regulation. Those countries that have followed such a prescription have had long periods of economic growth; for those who have not, economic growth has been much smaller. Evidence abounds as one compares the low tax-free enterprise economies such as Japan and many Pacific Rim countries with the high tax-big government economies such as most of Europe.

Secondly, it is important to open up economic opportunities for those in poverty by reducing the vast array of legal impediments that block entry into enterprise and occupations. It is a monumental tragedy that many poor today could be gainfully employed but are not because the law essentially blocks their progress. This occurs in a variety of ways and is often referred to as occupational licensure. It occurs when a number of requirements are mandated to enter an enterprise or occupation. These can be in the form of licenses, education requirements, zoning ordinances, building codes, proficiency tests and certification. It has been shown by many scholars over and over again that the real intent of these regulations has been not so much to protect the public but to protect those presently employed against newcomers.

This has grave consequences for the poor because many of them are newcomers. The last thing they need are regulations that limit occupational choice. For example, in the taxicab industry only three major metropolitan areas allow relatively free access into the market. In New York, for example, it takes $60,000 to purchase a taxicab "medallion" to operate a taxicab. This has the effect of excluding the entry of poor individuals in a market where entry costs would be ordinarily quite small. In Washington, D.C. where the market is relatively open, a high percentage of blacks and minorities (estimates are about 70%) own and operate cabs. In the plumbing and electrician fields, licensure has been used by craft unions to restrict entry. With entry governed by the craft unions, the number of job openings has been restricted by examinations that have often discriminated against blacks. Over 500 occupations are governed by such restrictions.

These restrictions apply not only to occupations but to the development of neighborhood associations. In a study by Robert Woodson, it was shown that the ability of private local groups to start up day care centers in urban ghetto areas was substantially retarded by zoning ordinances and building codes. It is somewhat of an anomaly that we are willing to spend a great deal on federal welfare but then turn around and deny opportunities to poor people through restrictive licensure. It is almost as if many middle class citizens are willing to bribe the poor with welfare money so that they can keep the poor away from middle class occupations.

Third, an important initiative is to establish a youth opportunity wage. Minimum wages have been responsible for a substantial portion of minority unemployment. When a youth is prohibited from working at $2.00 an hour, who is responsible for the job experience that is lost, the pride that can be developed from the experience, the respect and punctuality that can be instilled through such employment and the skills that can be developed to move up the job ladder? The truth is that the faster a poor person can get some kind of job experience, the faster he can gain the skill to move up.

My father grew up in a working class neighborhood in Camden, New Jersey, during the Depression. His most fond memories come from the variety of jobs he took as a youngster at very low wages. The many experiences he encountered and the discipline of getting up and going to work were indispensable to his future success. I think that is the reason that when he lost complete use of his right hand in an industrial accident in 1960, he was back at work in six months, never took a dime of welfare and complained to virtually no one.

Fourth, it is also useful to provide incentives for business development in ghetto neighborhoods. The most widely discussed option is the enterprise zone. Although there are some genuine fiscal problems with the approach, on balance enterprise zones can contribute a great deal. They have achieved considerable success at the state level. By reducing regulatory barriers, re-channeling public investment in more useful ways and providing tax incentives, enterprise zones are an important policy tool.

Creating Motivation and Ability

In order to create motivation and abilities for those in poverty to participate in the private sector, reform of existing welfare programs are required. There are two major problems: administration and disincentives. Many are beginning to notice that many federal programs do not serve poor people well. This is an age-old problem with public bureaucracy. Bureaucratic inertia makes it possible for programs to exist even though they are both inefficient and ineffective. As a consequence, there is a greater need for more poor people to become more involved in the process with greater responsibility put in their hands. Several strategies merit consideration.

First, the new emphasis placed on mediating structures is quite important. The approach is in many respects a private sector initiative. It is, in effect, the privatization of social programs. The approach is to give individuals and local associations more autonomy over decision making, in some cases, without substantial or any public subsidy. It is in some ways a market response to social problems. The House of Umoja in Philadelphia is a prime illustration of volunteer action on the part of individuals to solve youth crime problems. The Kenilworth project in Washington, DC, illustrates the success of private tenant management, and Homes for Black Children in Detroit shows how a private initiative reformed foster care problems. In each case public bureaucracy and regulations was circumvented by private initiatives. In each case, the results were strikingly better.

The success of these private initiatives should be given a further boost. They operate on a well established principle; when individuals are responsible for their own actions and investments, they put out the effort until they find something that works. Reducing regulatory barriers and providing legislation for the use of vouchers can greatly accelerate the trend.

Secondly, some attention should be given to the disincentives created by the interaction of the tax code and welfare benefits. The interaction of the two creates enormous disincentives to work. While all agree that it is humane to help out those in poverty, it is also humane to develop a system that does not trap individuals into poverty. Some thought in the future should be devoted to reforming the welfare system so that those who are able to take a job will do so when they crop up. This is not only fair to those who refuse welfare and work at modest wages, but it is helpful to those who have the ability to help themselves.

Lastly, the business sector has also played an important charitable role in reducing poverty. Many corporations and small businesses have established a variety of programs to help train, motivate and provide services to those in poverty. In fact, this private charity has increased considerably over the past five years. It is possible that we can learn from the more successful cases and incorporate this knowledge to reform the existing system. However, it should be realized that there are limits to how far we can travel this road. The prime objective of business is to satisfy its owners, employees and customers. Placing additional requirements on business only makes it harder for firms to compete and the economy grow.

POSITIVE REFORMS FOR FUTURE WELFARE POLICY

Rep. Jim Courter

As this country and indeed much of the world climbs out of the economic hole we had fallen into in the last decade and as the pace of economic growth increases over the rest of the 1980s and in the last decade of the century, we have to pay more attention, not less, to the problems of those who are not participating in prosperity. We are moving forward, and we must be sure we don't leave anyone behind.

Republicans and Democrats, liberals and conservatives, in a broad representation of the spectrum are offering a number of very different specific plans and ideas on welfare reform in the next decade.

Not so long ago people used to say that the conservatives couldn't care less about the poor, and the liberals care about them so much they don't want them to become rich. This view is disappearing rapidly and despite the differences in policy specifics, I think a new national consensus has been evolving. There is increasing agreement that the primary goal of welfare policy should be the reduction, even the elimination, of poverty as a way of life, that redistribution for the sake of redistribution is not enough, and indeed leaves the needy no better off than they were. Fighting poverty is not passe. Moreover, this consensus, in my view, extends to some of the principles that should go into welfare planning for the future. Basic is the recognition that, although massive government resource programs like the Great Society were well intentioned, they could not help but generate problems as intractable as those they were supposed to solve.

Welfare, you can say, is a public expression of compassion—but compassion is an individual, personalized sentiment. It expresses itself best when the relationship between those who give and those who are in need is personalized and close. This is why public assistance is better handled on lower levels of government, and improved even more by the involvement of people in their private capacities, in the so-called voluntary sector. No doubt massive federal programs can mobilize massive resources, but the cost, for instance, in the depersonalization of the family, which is the basic building block for all of our social principles—including compassion—is prohibitive. How can we be concerned about the poor if we undermine the foundation of that concern which is the family? By the end of this decade I expect the integrity of the family to be the center of America's welfare policy.

Scott Fitzgerald once said to Ernest Hemingway, "You know, the rich are different from us," and Hemingway said, "That's right. They have more money than we do." We are just relearning a very old lesson, that the poor respond to incentives just as the rich do.

More than a decade ago, the United States declared a war on hunger and poverty to help those people who could not afford the basic essentials most Americans enjoy. Massive public welfare programs were designed to subsidize the poor family's income so they could put food on the table.

What happened was that social spending in the federal budget exploded. Congress consistently underestimated the cost of the Food Stamp and other welfare programs. But, as the *New York Times* once editorialized, "Few social programs have so altered the conditions of American life as have food stamps. Until these federal coupons were introduced during the 60's, many poor people went hungry."

Virtually all Americans today agree that those who really need help should not be made to go without food, housing, or clothing.

But somewhere along the line, a number of individuals began to take advantage of the loopholes in these federally subsidized programs. More and more Americans are souring on a system that allows those who are not in need to live off the public treasury and which does little to encourage and assist able-bodied, employable people to work.

One great step toward alleviating this problem would be a federal workfare plan which would require unemployed, able-bodied adults to work in public sevice jobs for the value of their benefits. Such a program would affect recipients of food stamps, public subsidized housing, and welfare. Participation in such a program would not be required of any individual who is either under the age of 18 or over 65, or is disabled, or is regularly employed outside the program for at least forty hours a week, or is the person basically responsible for the care of a very young child.

A federal workfare program would add incentive for persons to look for a permanent job and, at the same time, would provide valuable on-the-job experience. In one community which tested such a program, for example, one man who was interested in electronics chose to work for his benefits by repairing the town's police car radios. His experience encouraged him eventually to find a position in an electrical repair shop.

This program would enable the hardcore unemployed to move into the economic mainstream and gain the satisfaction of contributing to the community. The community, in turn, also benefits from the work.

A small scale workfare program was begun a few years ago in my state of New Jersey, in Bordentown, when the mayor and town officials, fed up with the skyrocketing costs and red tape of a federal program, pulled the town off the state's general assistance program. The thirty-four people then on welfare were asked to reapply and were told they would have to work in order to collect benefits. Only four reapplied. Eventually, only one person remained on the welfare roll.

Nationwide studies were conducted some time ago under the auspices of the House Agriculture Committee, which tested a workfare project under which recipients of food stamps had to complete a certain number of hours in a public service job. It was soon discovered that close to fifty percent did not sign up when they were told they would have to work for their food stamps. They apparently did not want food stamps if they had to work for them. Thirteen percent were stimulated to find jobs on their own, and twenty percent said they benefitted from the experience and training of a public service job and enjoyed making a contribution to their community.

Across-the-board workfare would assist those who really need it and would weed out those who are taking advantage of the system's loopholes and effectively stealing finite resources from the genuine needy. This proposal would also assure taxpayers that their tax dollars are being allocated justly and fairly, not wasted.

Still, public service employment only makes sense as a transition to private sector work. In the 99th Congress, we advanced the most important poverty reduction, incentive-based ideas perhaps since the early New Deal. The House signalled the importance of establishing enterprise zones in our inner cities by passing legislation authorizing the administration to designate up to one hundred enterprise zones. The day before, the House took the unprecedented step of passing an amendment allowing H.U.D. to offer tenants in public housing projects the right to buy their homes at huge discounts with guaranteed low rate mortgages. Because I had fought hard to pass the amendment, which was co-authored by Congressman Jack Kemp and Delegate Walter Fauntroy, I will outline its purpose in greater detail as a prime example of consensus-style, family-oriented welfare reform.

The Home Ownership Amendment, as a prime example of family-centered welfare reform, was a radical breakthrough. It was radical in the manner the Homestead Bill following the Civil War was radical. At that time thousands of impoverished citizens were given an opportunity they could hardly have imagined they would ever have, a chance to own their own piece of property on the frontier and to extend the boundaries of civilization westward. Like that breakthrough program, the housing amendment proposed much the same thing in America's inner cities.

The secret of this privatization idea is that it provides a major new incentive for the poor to take advantage of employment opportunities to make this lifetime chance at the American dream a real possibility.

My own district is not one with a great deal of public housing, but New Jersey has numerous inner city areas that desperately need an alternative to public tenement homes. Any member of Congress from an inner city district well knows how much time and effort are spent on problems of conflicting residency claims, nonpayment of rents, nonresponding bureaucrats, and on all the social problems associated with living in a residential area which can be described in one word: despair.

What exactly is the problem? Some blame the public housing authorities, but the problem isn't really that. Like most public employees, the authorities' staffs are conscientious but they are literally swamped by the flood of complaints and problems. Nor is it the residents who are the problem. They don't like living with broken windows, littered halls, elevators that don't work, and drugs everywhere you look any more than anyone else—and in truth the residents want to get out as soon as possible. For them, public housing projects are not a home; they are more than a little like a jail.

Not long ago I travelled to the Soviet Union. Public housing there by definition is the rule, not the exception. One thing noticeable about Moscow high-rises is that they are all in conditions of terrible disrepair—broken windows, collapsing steps, shoddy maintenance—all of Moscow looks like an American inner city housing project. And it is not just poor families who live there—some have fairly good incomes. Poverty *per se* has little to do with the problems of upkeep.

The real problem is that public "property" is no one's property—it is what used to be called a "common," a word meaning the opposite of "property"—where no one has any incentive to improve the situation. With the Kemp-Fauntroy Amendment we offered residents for the first time something new, a reason for having pride in their homes, a reason to take hope instead of despair.

Let me be clear about a few matters some might be legitimately concerned about. This privatization proposal puts no one out of their home. Anyone who can not or does not wish to buy would remain there as long as they want, just as before. This proposal is not an effort to eliminate public housing for the needy. It does nothing to prevent Congress from meeting the need for more public housing in the future.

We are trying to provide an alternative for those who can take advantage of it, for the working poor. It may well be that this private home of their own will be the greatest asset the working poor will ever have in their lives. It will be the one thing they can really be proud of. Just think about the effect of private home ownership and the pride it represents on the children of the poor, what it means to them in self-respect, future-orientation, and the desire to save and invest. I believe this is one opportunity for black persons and minorities in our inner cities that Congress must address if Congress has any serious interest in solving the problems of the poor.

Unfortunately the Housing Privatization Amendment did not get through the Senate in 1986, but I have no doubt it will be offered again in the future until passage is completed. The 99th Congress, however, did pass the most dramatic tax reform since the income tax was created in 1913, doubling personal exemptions, removing millions of working poor families from the income tax rolls, and slashing the top tax rate to twenty-seven percent. These changes alone can reach down to the deepest levels of despair among the poor and open up opportunities to improve their lives and the lives of their families in a way which many perhaps never even dreamed was possible. I would certainly support a further increase in the personal deduction to four or five thousand dollars. In fact I anticipate this additional pro-family, anti-poverty tax code amendment to be introduced in the future.

We Americans realize that economic prosperity is only a part of a deeper kind of well-being. Jobs, economic opportunity, a growing economy are good for things beyond themselves—they are good for society, for charity and philanthropy, for the family, and for the individual—they are good, in other words, for developing human potential, for what used to be called *character development.* The so-called "social issues" of today can find common ground with the new direction of welfare policy, in concentrating on strengthening the family. Perhaps the cruellest aspect of poverty as a way of life and of the misguided programs sometimes offered to deal with it is that they create a kind of impoverishment of the spirit as the cost of trying to reduce material impoverishment. But welfare literally means to "fare well," to improve oneself in body and soul. I believe that in the coming years there must and will be a consensus on the idea that welfare must be measured by its effects on people's character as much as its improvement of their economics.

RENEWING GOVERNMENT PROGRAMS FOR FUTURE NEEDS

Rep. Sander Levin

When AFDC was established in 1935, it was seen as solely an income assistance program. Despite piecemeal and often inconsistent attempts over the last twenty years, we've failed to link AFDC recipients to work and training programs aimed at helping them gain economic independence. Now, with increasing need, new understandings, and national attention focused on the challenge of bringing new opportunities to the disadvantaged, *the time has come to make job training and preparation a top priority for the AFDC system.* We must not continue to reduce the resources or threaten the program authorizations that make training and job preparation possible for AFDC recipients. Instead, *we must weld AFDC to proven programs that enable recipients to leave the welfare rolls and join payrolls.*

We now know enough to create a successful program. We can build off the proven records of the twenty-six states that operate WIN Demonstration programs; we can build off of the authoritative evaluations prepared by the Manpower Development Research Corporation; and we can build from the recommendations proffered by the National Governors' Association, the American Public Welfare Association, the Children's Defense

Fund, and many other groups whose hands-on experience has shown what works and what doesn't.

The time for reform is now. Right now the average monthly AFDC caseload is close to eleven million people, mostly women and children. Since 1979, child poverty has increased 31%, the sharpest increase since poverty statistics have been collected. We need to do something now to give greater opportunity to the millions of poor families receiving welfare payments and a brighter future to the one out of five American children who live in poverty. We need welfare reform now, not because we wish to blame those in poverty or force them to exchange their welfare benefits for make-work that leads them neither out of poverty nor towards new skills that can guide them out of a dead end road. We need to act now because we know some of the answers that can help families now.

We know the difficulties those receiving welfare face—and I mean the adults, not the children, who represent two thirds of all recipients. We know that one half of all AFDC recipients are high school drop outs. Many are functionally illiterate and for them, finding a job is not as simple as skimming the want ads or perusing the yellow pages for suitable employers—they can't read or understand either one. They often need remedial education and the opportunity to finish school if they are to succeed at any level in the job market.

Even more important, we know that female heads of households, aged 25 to 34, can earn enough to keep a family of three out of poverty in 80% of all traditionally male occupations but in only 45% of all traditionally female occupations. For a single woman raising her children this fact mandates that she find not simply a job paying the minimum wage that guarantees that she and her family will remain mired in poverty; she needs a job that can bring her an adequate income and at least some health benefits for her family. We should not expect mothers of young children to give up their Medicaid benefits for a job that does nothing about health coverage. In addition, child care and transportation assistance must be available to those in training.

Poor women need more than simple job hunting skills; they need the training that will let them enter the job market primed to find and keep a good job in an expanding field. To give them less is to only hold out false hope and, for many, a return to the AFDC rolls.

We have all heard much about the success of the Massachusetts ET Choices program. Massachusetts is one of many states that has had success in helping thousands of AFDC recipients leave welfare for work.

In 1984, my home state began the Michigan Opportunity and Skills Training Program (MOST), relying in large part on WIN funds and WIN Demonstration authority. When the program began, Michigan's AFDC caseload stood at 245,924. In less than two years, better than 55,000 people found work after going through some type of education and skill training. Approximately one half found jobs that offered health benefits.

To prepare people for jobs, the MOST program offers welfare recipients a variety of training opportunities. Since 47% of all MOST participants begin the program without a high school diploma, general education is a necessity. Many participants also take advantage of job-specific vocational education programs and community college courses. Participants are trained for clerical positions, word processing, food service occupations, auto mechanics and a variety of other growing occupations. For those already job-ready there are three separate forms of job search—job club, job seeking and job development—each tailored to the specific needs of specific participants. And for those in need of job experience, in order to develop improved work habits and attitudes or to maintain or upgrade existing skills, the Community Work Experience Program offers a valuable opportunity.

To insure that all recipients can maintain their participation, MOST allocates substantial funds for child care and transportation particularly important for rural participants. The program is not cheap, approximately $40 million a year—$18 million from WIN and the balance from state revenues. But it serves a monthly average of 41,000 welfare recipients and, as of August 1985, had already saved $36 million in reduced welfare payments. As the long term effects of those initial savings accumulate, that dollar total will rise.

Based on the results of Michigan's project and the many other successful AFDC work, training, and education programs I was fortunate enough to review as Chair of the Democratic Caucus Task Force on Job Training, we put together a proposal that builds on the proven record. We combine the best parts of several programs while maintaining each state's right and need to tailor their program to meet their particular situation. The result is *WORC*—the *Work Opportunities and Retraining Compact of 1986.*

WORC contains six key elements.

1. *A comprehensive plan to link Welfare and Training.*

   All states would be required to develop a comprehensive employment and training plan for welfare recipients. The effect would be to consolidate the many separate funding and program authorities that now exist under Title IV. The bill would also require that this training program be developed in partnership with other state and local agencies responsible for job training and education including programs administered under the Job Training Partnership Act, Employment Service, vocational education, local education agencies and community colleges.

2. *Mandatory registration, counseling, and assessment for all non-exempt AFDC recipients.*

   Out of the assessment and counseling process will come a job preparation plan for every individual. States would be encouraged to promote the voluntary participation of persons exempted from work-related requirements.

3. *Education and training options must be provided.*

   States would be required to offer education and training options to those who need such opportunities to become job ready. All of the employment activities currently permitted under WIN/WIN Demonstrations, JTPA, and under all other AFDC work program authorities would be funded, as would any other program leading to employment.

4. *Child care and transportation assistance available to those participants who need it at all points during the program.*

5. *Adequate resources to fund a comprehensive program.*

Funding would be provided on a 70% federal and 30% state matching rate for all training and education costs and in the outyears would be raised to 75/25 where states exceeded performance standards. Administrative and support service costs such as child care and transportation would be funded at a 50% federal and 50% state matching rate.

6. *Performance measured not by simple participation but by measured outcomes.*

Building on the JTPA experience, both national and state performance standards would be set. States that met or exceeded performance standards would have a lower match rate. Standards would be developed by the Office of Technology Assessment in consultation with the Secretary of Labor and with the advice of state officials and other experts. These standards will include such measures as job placement rates, job retention, reduction of welfare costs and caseloads, education improvements and percent of jobs that provide employer financed health care benefits. Performance standards will give credit to programs that help those with the greatest barriers to employment and take into account the unemployment rate in each state. These performance standards should be coordinated with JTPA standards.

Over the last few years we have learned a painful lesson; a rising tide does not lift all boats. And some people, we have also discovered or rediscovered, don't even have a boat to get into. But with *WORC* we can build a national program that offers those in poverty new opportunity. We can help those who are stuck on the bottom to find their own way up and out.

The 100th Congress is very likely to pass the first meaningful welfare reform in twenty years. Legislation incorporating many of the features of WORC is currently being considered in both the House and the Senate.

CHALLENGES FOR TOMORROW

Rep. Robert S. Walker

Few issues have baffled policymakers more than that of real welfare reform. Fewer issues capture as well the essence of the relationship between the government and the individual. It does us little good to simply recite the dry litany of statistics illustrating the colossal failure of the War on Poverty. The legacy is a human tragedy, a modern day drama playing itself out in every community, town and city in America. The story goes far beyond mere numbers. One need only to walk a few blocks from the Capitol, just out of the shadow of the building where most of the welfare reform laws and policies have been launched with all the best of intentions, to see firsthand the pain of hopelessness and despair etched on the faces of dozens of jobless men and women, milling about with nothing to do, having no purpose in life other than collecting that next welfare check, their self-esteem melting away with each passing day.

The sheer scale of the assault on the poverty problem takes your breath away. The federal government alone has invested billions of dollars in trying to eliminate poverty. Yet by even the most optimistic measure, the poverty level in this country is mired at about 10 percent of the population, reflecting millions of people caught in the quicksand of federal policies and programs intended to get them into the mainstream of the American economy.

Just by way of contrast, the federal government spent roughly the same amount of money, in constant dollars, on the NASA program and on job training programs during the 1960s. The goal of the NASA program, clearly specified, was to put a man on the Moon. The goal of the job training programs was to move people out of poverty. One was a fabulous success. The other was a failure. The answer to the difference is that in the NASA program we had a clearly identified, simple strategy, one that drew from the values and aspirations of the best that our nation had to offer. In the other, we threw money and complicated programs at the problem, and forgot about the social values that we were trying to encourage. Almost to add insult to injury, the NASA program not only put a man on the Moon, but by virtue of its tremendous success it spun-off tens of thousands of new jobs in the process, many more times than were ever created by the federal job training effort.

That bankruptcy of thought and vacuum of leadership in the welfare debate creates a remarkable opportunity to reorder both the welfare reform debate and, along with it, the modern welfare state. Our strategy should be simple, and it should emphasize values, social obligations in exchange for assistance. It's exactly as Charles Murray says, who ends his book, *Losing Ground,* with:

"The real contest about the direction of social policy is not between people who want to cut budgets and people who want to help. When reforms finally do occur, they will happen not because stingy people have won, but because generous people have stopped kidding themselves."

The liberals have stopped kidding themselves, and the stingy people lost. They always will.

The first step toward taking advantage of this rare opportunity is to recognize that part of the problem is us. For too long conservatives have been cast as the villains in the welfare reform play, slashing budgets and throwing little old ladies and children out into the street. Republicans and conservatives have let the Democrats and the liberals paint us into a corner as a bunch of stone-hearted, flinty-eyed accountants, interested only in keeping welfare budget costs down and caseload numbers to a minimum, with no comprehensive alternatives of our own, save welfare queen stories and other anecdotes.

But I want to underscore my point: we need to go further. We need to take the offensive, aggressively. The first phase of our strategy is to shuck off that image of being a party of bean counters, green-eye shade accountants. Our welfare vision should encompass a bold, sweeping strategy, driven by values, not costs. It should be a system that places a premium on the values that the American people hold dear: opportunity, work, community-based decision-making, and family responsibility to society.

To win this fight we need to move to a higher level than the tactical level. We need to regroup, lay out a new strategy emphasizing our strengths, our principles and our values. Part of the answer lies in the nature of the character of the American people themselves. The American people are a generous people, of that there can be no question. At the same time, they have certain core values that they themselves believe in, and expect everyone else, especially their neighbors, to abide by also. Those values are hard work, thrift, and certain standards of socially acceptable behavior.

One of the faults of liberalism's attack on poverty is that it has tilted too far toward tapping the generosity of the American people, while ignoring the exchange of certain values in return for that generosity.

The first item on our agenda should be to propose a giant block grant that combines $100 to $150 billion worth of the federal government's existing low-income programs into one funding stream and then sends the money directly to local communities and counties for spending as they see fit within certain broad categories, such as housing, food, medical, and educational assistance. Once the block grant is in place, we can then actively explore follow-on strategies aimed at turning back and then leaving revenue sources for these programs at the point where the programs are administered.

But in the meantime, the mega-block grant meets three essential criteria for establishing an alternative, values-based assistance system.

The first test the block grant meets is that it moves the administrative responsibility as far away from Washington as possible and back into the community. Ideally, programs, should be run at the community or neighborhood level, and staffed by residents of that community.

All existing benefit delivery systems should be consolidated into one office, creating a one-stop facility for recipients. Eligibility standards under the block grant should be as localized as much as possible to emphasize local accountability. It should be clearly specified that the block grant can only be spent to meet the needs of low-income people, as defined by that locality's or state's standard of need.

That would correct one of the major logistical problems with the current welfare system, which is a patchwork of crazy-quilt offices, buildings and other locations that do nothing but confuse, frustrate and alienate recipients. Instead of spending hours and even days trooping around to the right building or office, time which could be better spent working, recipients should be able to stop at one location and inquire about a wide array of possible benefits, ranging from housing, education, medical or just general purpose assistance.

Another advantage of the one-stop center is that recipients could have their benefit packages tailored to meet their specific needs. Too often under the current system, the recipient finds a little bit of a lot of different programs that might help, but no one program that fits his or her predicament precisely. As a result, the recipient falls through the cracks of an overly rigid, inflexible system. The one-stop concept strips away that inflexibility, and allows administrators to design benefit packages that meet the needs of recipients exactly.

The system could be further humanized by calling these centers "family centers" and it is through them that all benefits for that particular neighborhood should flow. Calling them family centers sends the subtle, yet important, message that the purpose of these facilities is to help families and encourage family stability, an element sadly lacking in our current administrative set-up.

Second, family centers should be required to cooperate as much as possible with community organizations, churches and other voluntary organizations in order to minimize bureaucracy. In addition, these volunteer groups would be able to fill whatever gaps might exist in government efforts. For instance, they could be used as child care centers for working mothers receiving family assistance, provide needed moral guidance for pregnant, unwed teenagers, children involved in crime, or provide job training for other recipients.

Encouraging consolidation of programs would eliminate many of the horrible mismatches we now see happening with more and more frequency. We've virtually doubled food stamp program spending over the last decade, and still we hear reports about hunger in America. We're in the midst of one of the biggest home building booms since World War II, and still there are reports of people who have no place to live. We've created almost 10 million new jobs since 1980, and still there are people who can't find a job.

To vent their frustration, we see millions of people taking part in events like Hands Across America, Farm-Aid, and Live-Aid. Millions and millions of Americans want to help. They just don't know how. The problem is too distant. Or too complex. Offering them a hands-on chance to help people in their communities, as the community-based block grant would do, would help focus that emotion and energy in socially constructive ways that really help solve the problem.

Running the programs at the community level will foster an environment of creativity and innovation in administering social programs. Local officials have a much better idea of how to meet local needs than do federal bureaucrats laboring under a mountain of regulations and red tape. Local governments will naturally experiment with better ways to achieve the same goals. Already we're seeing examples of localities taking up the challenge. Not too far from Washington, D.C., Prince George's County is setting up an educational assistance fund for disadvantaged students, in order to help fill gaps left by federal cutbacks.

In addition, the block grant would create a much needed incentive for local officials to contract out, or privatize, many services that can be run more efficiently or effectively by private agencies. For instance, a private temporary employment agency may be able to train welfare recipients for worthwhile jobs more effectively than current job training programs can. By the same token, it may be more efficient to contract out food delivery services to a private food service company that already serves cafeterias or businesses in the community.

The second test the mega-block grant approach meets is that it should be structured so that it restores the primacy of the family over the state in government policy.

Michael Novak, looking back at the past twenty-five years of government social policy, comments that social policy has been centered around two poles: the individual, which is where a lot of conservatives, particularly libertarians, place most of their emphasis, and the state, which is where most liberals turn for answers.

Focusing too much on either of these two poles, however, creates disorder. Emphasizing the individual can produce chaos because it tends to ignore the inherent responsibilities of individuals to society. Concentrating on the state for solutions smothers pluralism and fosters dependency. Taken together, neither truly meets the needs of society, particulary in helping to lift people out of poverty. And that's precisely the situation we've got in today's welfare culture: a system run amok which delivers services through the state to individuals, while producing disorder and a lack of social responsibility.

The answer is to stress the importance of the family as an intermediary between the individual and the state, but with primacy over both. The role of the state should be to empower people, not enslave them or make them dependent on the state. Since the 1950s, we've made great strides in empowering people politically, extending the right to vote to everyone in the country. Unfortunately we have paid less attention to empowering people economically, giving them a stake in the system and in their own futures.

The role of the family is to take the best characteristics of the individual and meld them together to form something stronger than individuals can form on their own. The state's role should be to assure stronger families.

The most sweeping reform we could make in governmental policy today is already happening: it is the tax reform revolution. In one fell swoop that bill removes six million low-income families from the tax rolls, making it infinitely easier for them to escape the poverty trap. It eases the oppressive tax burden on family creation by doubling the personal exemption, and rewards family stability by encouraging growth and the creation of jobs. Perhaps best of all, it restores children to their rightful place in society, not a burden to be feared, as many modern day Malthusians tend to view them, but as a source of new wealth, in the Biblical sense, for society

Remaining family disincentives contained in existing welfare programs, like the AFDC program, should be removed. Again, administering block grants at the local level will eliminate many of those distortions. But other specific initiatives worth pursuing might be options such as denying rent subsidies to unwed, pregnant teenagers with known parents. That would eliminate the incentive for teenagers to move to housing projects to have their babies. There are many, many other initiatives that can be pursued, once local officials get the authority they need and once recipients know that the welfare system can be humanized; that there's more to the system than numbers on a check; that there are people from their community, neighbors, who are trying to help them get out of poverty.

The final test met by the block grant approach is that specific conditions should be set as a condition for receiving aid. For instance, at a minimum recipients should be required to work for their benefits. Recipients should be required to work not as a punishment, or to demean them, but to instill in them the value of hard work and the value of making a contribution to the community. Or people receiving housing assistance should be required to make improvements to their house or apartment as a condition for receiving that assistance. They could be given an option to buy their residence after a sufficient period of time. Medical assistance could be provided on the condition that recipients not engage in drug abuse, or that they participate in a preventative health program. It could also be provided on the condition that unwed teenagers obtain counseling from nongovernmental sources, such as the church. Educational assistance could be provided on the grounds that applicants meet certain academic standards, such as SAT scores or grade point averages, or even minimum attendance standards. In short, we should expect nothing less from people receiving public assistance than we expect of ourselves or our neighbors.

Our welfare system vision must be one that stresses the principle that recipients of aid must return something of value to the community in exchange for assistance.

After all, what we're really talking about doing is instilling the Lockean version of the social contract in poverty programs, that compact that became the basis of our country's Declaration of Independence.

Remember, what Locke said was that all men existed in a state of nature and that the price for them moving out of the state of nature into civilization was to assume certain collective obligations and abide by socially responsible standards of behavior. "For, when any number of men have, by the consent of every individual, made a community, they have thereby made that community one body, with a power to act as one body, which is only by the will and determination of the majority," Locke wrote, "thus every man, by consenting with others to make one body politic under one government, puts himself under an obligation to everyone of that society to submit to the determination of the majority . . . or else this original compact . . . would signify nothing, and be no compact if he be left free and under no other ties than he was in before in the state of nature."

Social obligation. Civic responsibility. Returning something of value to the community. Those should be the pillars for our strategy. It's a message we should take straight to the people, doing an end run around the Washington establishment and elites. As we have recently celebrated the 100th anniversary of the unveiling of the Statue of Liberty, and should remember that our forebears worked themselves out of poverty, improved their lot in life by working hard, relying on their family and leaving their community in better shape than they found it.

The time has come to begin the debate anew, to develop a positive strategy that cuts at last the shackles of bondage holding people in poverty. The intellectual battle will not be unlike the drive for emancipation in the 1800s, a fight that gave birth to the Republican Party. As Abraham Lincoln, the embodiment of both the fight for abolition and the founding of the Republican Party, said during the Lincoln-Douglas debates:

> "What contributes the bulwark of our liberty and independence? Our reliance is in the love of liberty which God has planted in us. Our defense is the spirit which prized liberty as the heritage of all men . . . Destroy this spirit and you have planted the seeds of despotism at your own door. Familiarize yourselves with the chains of bondage and you prepare your own limbs to wear them. Accustomed to trample on the rights of others, you have lost the genius of your own independence and become the fit subjects of the first cunning tyrant who rises among you."

The Civil War was fought over the question of political empowerment. This struggle will be fought on the battleground of economic empowerment, of giving people in poverty a stake in our economic system.

A values-based welfare system emphasizing community, personal accountability and local decision-making which encourages values like strong families, work, social responsibility and obligation is but the first step on the long road to economic freedom and independence for millions of people now in poverty. But it must be done. Economic growth and prosperity without the full participation of all in society is not enough. We owe it not only to ourselves, but more importantly to future generations.

Politically such an initiative could do for building a new majority what the New Deal did for building the liberal coalition. But even better than that, we will have come to grips with one of the most troubling domestic problems of our time, and we will have done it in a way that ensures that we will have left our society stronger and our country a better place to live than when we found it. We will have given everyone who wants it a stake in our system a chance. And we will have given everyone who wants their share of the American Dream a piece of the future.

CONTRIBUTORS

CARL A. ANDERSON is a Special Assistant to the President for Public Liaison and head of the Domestic Issues Division of the Office of Public Liaison. Previously, he served in the White House Office of Policy Development where his responsibilities included co-chairing the White House Working Group on Family Issues. From 1981 to 1983, Mr. Anderson served as legal advisor in the Office of the Secretary of Health and Human Services.

BLANCHE BERNSTEIN is currently a consultant in social welfare policy and administration, and has previously served as Commissioner of the New York City Human Resources Department of Social Services and Deputy Commissioner of the New York State Department of Social Services for the Division. Her most recent book is *Saving a Generation* (1986) which examines the special problems of female-headed families.

ROBERT B. CARLESON is chairman of Robert B. Carleson and Associates, a Washington, DC consulting firm. From 1981 to 1984 he served as Special Assistant to the President for Policy Development. He was previously the U.S. Commissioner of Welfare in the Department of Health, Education and Welfare, and Director of the California State Department of Social Welfare.

JIM COURTER (R-NJ) was elected to the U.S. House of Representatives in 1978, and is a member of the Aging Committee and the Armed Services Committee. He was the founder of the first Legal Aid Society office in Warren County, NJ, and also served in the Peace Corps.

JAMES S. DENTON is the President of the National Forum Foundation, a Washington, DC public policy research and education organization. He has written and edited essays and articles on policy issues, including *The Fairness Debate*. He has also testified before the U.S. Senate Finance Committee's subcommittee hearings on welfare reform and child support enforcement.

WILLIAM J. GRIBBIN is widely published in the field of American history and social commentary. Dr. Gribbin served as the Deputy Director of the White House Office of Legislative Affairs from 1981 to 1982, and was Editor-in-Chief of the Republican Platform in 1984.

LESLIE LENKOWSKY is President of the Institute for Educational Affairs, a non-profit organization in Washington, DC, devoted to enhancing innovative thinking in higher education and philanthropy. He is also an adjunct professor of public policy at Georgetown University and on leave from the American Enterprise Institute. Dr. Lenkowsky is author of numerous articles and books, including *Politics, Economics, and Welfare Reform*.

SANDER MARTIN LEVIN (D-MI) was elected to the U.S. House of Representatives in 1982, and serves on House Committee on Banking, Finance and Urban Affairs, and on the Intergovernmental Relations and Human Resources Subcommittee of the Committee on Government Operations. He is also a member of the Select Committee on Children, Youth and Families.

GLENN C. LOURY is Professor of Political Economy at the Kennedy School of Government, Harvard University. Dr. Loury is author of numerous scholarly articles, and has held Ford Foundation and Guggenheim fellowships.

SENATOR DANIEL PATRICK MOYNIHAN (D-NY) has the distinction of serving in four successive administrations, under

Presidents Kennedy, Johnson, Nixon, and Ford. He also served as U.S. Ambassador to India and the United Nations. He is the author, co-author or editor of 14 books.

MICHAEL NOVAK holds the George F. Jewett Chair of Religion and Public Policy at the American Enterprise Institute in Washington, DC. He has written over twenty books in philosophy, theology, politics, economics, and culture. Dr. Novak is also author of more than two hundred articles and reviews.

JUNE O'NEILL is the Assistant Staff Director for Programs, Policy and Research at the U.S. Commission for Civil Rights. Previously, Dr. O'Neill directed a research program at the Urban Institute on the economics of women, income security programs, tax policy, and education. She is author of numerous essays and books.

WILLIAM ORZECHOWSKI is Director of Federal Budget Policy at the U.S. Chamber of Commerce in Washington, DC. Dr. Orzechowski has written widely and was professor of economics at George Mason University in Virginia from 1980-1984.

RICHARD VEDDER is Distinguished Professor of Economics at Ohio University, where he has been a member of the faculty since 1965. Dr. Vedder has written extensively on nineteenth and twentieth century American economic history as well as contemporary public policy issues.

ROBERT S. WALKER (R-PA) was elected to the U.S. House of Representatives in 1976, where he serves as Republican leader of the Intergovernmental Relations and Human Resources Subcommittee of the House Government Operations Committee. He was also appointed by the House of Representatives as Commissioner on Intergovernmental Relations.

JOHN C. WEICHER holds the F.K. Weyerhaeuser Chair in Public Policy Research at the American Enterprise Institute. In 1981 he served as Deputy Staff Director of the President's Commission on Housing, and also served at the U.S. Department of Housing and Urban Development. Dr. Weicher has written four books and numerous articles.